Jasper's

KITCHEN
COOKBOOK

ALSO BY JASPER J. MIRABILE, JR.

THE JASPER'S COOKBOOK

KITCHEN
COOKBOOK

ITALIAN RECIPES AND MEMORIES FROM
KANSAS CITY'S LEGENDARY RESTAURANT

JASPER J. MIRABILE, JR.

**Andrews McMeel
Publishing, LLC**

Kansas City • Sydney • London

09 10 11 12 13 RR2 10 9 8 7 6 5 4 3 2 1

ISBN-13: 978-0-7407-7862-9
ISBN-10: 0-7407-7862-5

Library of Congress Control Number: 2009923689

Cover photos © 2009 by Thomas Gibson
Book design by Kelly Ludwig

www.andrewsmcmeel.com
www.jasperskc.com

ATTENTION: SCHOOLS AND BUSINESSES
Andrews McMeel books are available at quantity discounts with bulk purchase for educational, business, or sales promotional use. For information, please write to: Special Sales Department, Andrews McMeel Publishing, LLC, 1130 Walnut Street, Kansas City, Missouri 64106.

CONTENTS

FOREWORD

Call him the king of Italian cuisine. The sovereign of slow food. The prince of locally produced ingredients. Call Jasper Mirabile, Jr., whatever you want to, as long as he calls you to dinner.

Because whatever Jasper's titles are in his vast fiefdom of food—educator, radio show host, world traveler, author, businessman—it's his passion for cooking that earns him the crown as one of the country's most respected and beloved chefs.

In fact, if you're lucky enough to live in Kansas City, you'll swear Jasper has a clone. Take a typical Saturday morning in July. There's Jasper, extolling the virtues of heirloom tomatoes at a farmer's market before heading to his regular gig as food guru on the *Live! From Jasper's Kitchen* radio show. By midafternoon, he's teaching a cooking class at a Hen House grocery store—where colorful jars of his divine pasta sauces line the shelves—before rushing back to his restaurant to host an event for a big-name cookbook author. Later, he oversees the kitchen of his award-winning dining room.

It's no secret to Jasper's legion of fans that he's incredibly generous with his time and talents. That generosity extends to sharing these recipes that have been passed down from family members and crafted from trips to the Mirabile homeland.

Jasper's passion for good food—and all the camaraderie and joy that accompanies it—is a gift. And now, by owning this cookbook, it's a gift you can share with the people you love.

—*Katie Van Luchene, executive editor of* Kansas City Magazine *and author of* The Insiders' Guide to Kansas City

A LOVE AFFAIR WITH JASPER'S

LOVE AT FIRST SIGHT

You can say that my "love affair" with Jasper's started the first day I laid eyes on Jasper Mirabile, Sr. I still remember that day like it was yesterday. I was just a teenager in high school, and I used to frequent a drugstore called Parview on Independence Avenue. Jasper worked there—it was one of his first jobs as a teenager. Jasper used to tell his friends at the soda fountain that he was going to marry Josephine Cropis someday.

Falling in Love

I graduated from Northeast High School in Kansas City, and Jasper graduated from De La-Salle Military School. He had a brand-new black Dodge and was the only person in the neighborhood with a car. Actually, it was his father's car, but I didn't know that at the time! I was going to the Gladstone Theatre, and Jasper asked me if I needed a ride. We talked that evening, and I fell in love with him. It was Easter time, and he told me he was on his way to play football at St. Mary's, in California. I heard nothing from him for a while, and I thought he had dumped me, but that summer he returned to Kansas City, and we began dating.

My Mother's Meatball Recipe

I must tell the truth. In the beginning, I thought Jasper was more interested in my mother's meatball recipe and her lemonade than he was in me. Seriously, I thought that was the only reason he called on me.

Too Busy to Propose

Jasper and I dated for six years. During that time he was very busy working at his father's bar, The Lucky Tavern at 12th and Troost, and attending school. We actually had to *schedule* time to be alone! It wasn't easy to get him to propose to me. His sense of responsibility and love of family were priorities for him. Family meant everything to Jasper then and until the day he passed.

Marriage: Food and Family

In 1953, we were married at St. John's Catholic Church and had a reception at the Town Hall. We had a big, wonderful Italian wedding that included family, friends, and, of course, food. There were tables full of cookies and family specialties, including a big festive dinner of spaghetti and meatballs. Early the next morning, at 1 a.m., we had breakfast at the Southern Mansion.

The next day, we left for New York in Jasper's new car, a yellow Pontiac convertible, with $1,400 in cash. Jasper was anxious for me to meet his New Jersey family and all the friends he had grown up with. I felt like Dorothy from *The Wizard of Oz*. I knew we weren't in Kansas (City) anymore, and I felt as though I'd just entered the Emerald City!

We stayed at the Waldorf Astoria, for $22 per night, and we stayed there only for 2 nights. I couldn't stand the hotel—I was the girl from Ord Street! What did I know back then? So we moved to another hotel and had a suite for $12 per night.

Jasper's Cousins

During our visit, I met Jasper's cousins, the Lombardinos. This was the first time I had met Paul and Christine Lombardino and their children, Carl and Marie. When we left their home, Christine told Jasper we would have gravy on Sunday. During the ride back to the city, I remember asking Jasper, "Why are we eating gravy?" Jasper laughed and said, "Josephine, gravy is what they call sauce here. We are going to eat pasta with gravy!"

Jasper took me to so many wonderful places during that trip. He took me to see *South Pacific* and *The King and I*. Jasper introduced me to every Broadway play and even the horse races. One night we won $100 at the races, so we had dinner at Mama Leone's.

THE PICNIC IN KANSAS CITY

We returned to Kansas City with $1.50! Jasper bought a loaf of bread and a pound of bologna, and we had a picnic the night before he went back to work. Jasper always liked picnics, and every trip we took after that he would stop at a local grocery and buy "picnic food." Even during our vacations to France and Italy in the seventies it was the highlight of the trip.

LIVING THE DREAM

After Jasper and I returned to Kansas City, he began living his dream. He worked at the Southern Mansion as a bartender and then purchased the Ship, at I-435 east of 11th Street, and worked that bar for a year. We lived with my in-laws until we bought our first home. After saving

$5,000, we purchased Rose's Bar at 75th Street and Wornall Road. Jasper later changed the name to Jasper's. His mama cooked the sauces, and I prepared boiled eggs for the bar. I was pregnant with Leonard, our first son, and a customer made eyes at me. Jasper put me on the bus and sent me home. From that day on, I took care of the books and house charges, made copies of the menus each day (on a hectograph machine), and raised three more children: Salvatore, James, and Jasper, Jr.

We lived on North Van Brunt, and one day Jasper asked me if I wanted to move to South Kansas City, to be closer to the restaurant. So in 1958 we moved to 109th Street and Wornall Road.

We never took a vacation until 1966, when we went to St. Louis. After that vacation, Jasper decided to close for two weeks every July to spend time with his family. The boys were growing up, and he wanted to see them more often. As the boys grew up, I stayed home and continued to do the book work. We were not wealthy by any means, and Jasper saved his money to update the restaurant and remodel it from time to time.

OUR FIRST TRIP TO ITALY

We started traveling in 1970 and took our first trip to Italy. We toured Rome and stayed with relatives in Sicily. Jasper took me to my family's hometown, Corleone, Sicily, to see my parents' birthplace, where they had lived until they immigrated to America in 1914.

Jasper and Josephine on vacation

We traveled to the French Riviera and Paris the same year. I will never forget how Jasper used to read every magazine and cookbook and research restaurants that he wanted to visit. I recall eating at a restaurant in Livorno, Italy, when Jasper discovered our most famous dish, Scampi alla Livornese.

I'll also never forget when Jasper and I ate Spaghetti Carbonara for the first time in Rome, where the dish was invented. He made us eat at the same restaurant three nights in a row so that he could determine the recipe. Finally, on our last night, he hollered out, "ONIONS! They caramelize the onions with a splash of sherry wine!" He was extremely gifted at picking apart a dish just by taste. He would then come home and experiment with the dish with our chef.

Jasper also loved marketing and advertising our restaurant. I swear that is where our youngest son gets his love for media and PR. Before the days of food critics, Jasper would invite writers to our home on Sundays to experience his new dishes. He was continually tweaking dishes, adding more basil, reducing with different types of wines, etc. He had an insatiable appetite for reading cookbooks, and he encouraged our boys to do the same.

When it came to schooling, Jasper was not formally trained in the restaurant business. He taught himself how to cook, work the floor, and run the office. He also had many devoted employees over the years.

That's my love affair with Jasper. It's a love affair with the man and his restaurant. Although he no longer physically occupies this world, his spirit lives on through his sons, their families, our talented chefs, and every dish that they prepare and serve to all of our devoted customers and friends.

We are so very fortunate to live our dream!

Josephine Mirabile
May 2009

Introduction

When it comes to feeding my passion, I rarely turn down anything, whether it's enjoying a great dish of pasta at my cousin's home in Sicily, eating a cannolo in Rome with friends, or writing this cookbook.

The recipes that you'll enjoy from *Jasper's Kitchen Cookbook* are like members of my own family because they all represent so much of my heritage. My nana's sauce that I learned how to make at her knee as a boy, dishes that my father perfected from our travels together, and, of course, Mama, who, to this day, I still learn new things from. We like to think that the wonderful experiences our friends have in the restaurant are because our customers are extensions of our family. So much of our Mirabile history has revolved around Jasper's that our customers couldn't help but be a part of our family! We're true Italians—we love life, and so much of it revolves around the table. My family and my restaurant are my life, my passion, my love.

I am involved locally with many groups, but my heart is with Slow Food Kansas City, a convivium I started in 2002. I love to support the local farmers and food artisans from the Midwest. To me, that is what it is all about—cooking and eating locally. We are fortunate to have some of the finest farmers, bakers, and artisans in the country. They fuel the creativity in my recipes and help me to continue the Italian tradition of eating what is in season and supporting local markets.

So, if you love Italian food, I hope you'll take these recipes and prepare them. But do not stop there. Continue on, add your favorite herb or fresh cheese, take your time, and experiment. For me, that is what it is all about! As you read our story and share these recipes with your friends and family, I wish you the best from all of us at Jasper's. And as my father would always say, *bere e mangiare bene*—drink and eat well!

Salute!

Jasper J. Mirabile, Jr.

CHAPTER 1

IN THE BEGINNING

Nana's father owned a bakery in Shreveport, Louisiana

IT STARTED WITH A DREAM

This story began more than a century ago, when my grandfather, Leonardo Mirabile, emigrated from Sicily to find a new beginning in America.

My father, Jasper, learned to cook from his mother, my nana, Josephine. When he was as young as eight years old, my father would cook pasta at home after school and place it in a basket on his bicycle and ride to the family grocery store in New Jersey to bring dinner to his mom and pop. When he came back home to Kansas City, met my mother, and together with his parents purchased Rose's, his critics said he would never make it "way out there" in Waldo in South Kansas City. It was the county line, and in 1954 that was the end of the old streetcar line—just way too far out to succeed.

In the beginning, my father used recipes from my nana. He didn't have the knowledge of accounting or staffing to run a business. What he did have was a dream—a dream to run the best restaurant in Kansas City and offer authentic Italian food. And he realized his dream. In 1996, more than forty years after opening Jasper's on April Fool's Day, 1954, he was inducted into the Distinguished Restaurants of North America (DiRoNA) Hall of Fame.

Many people do not know how my father struggled. In the early days, he didn't even have enough money to buy a lock for his apartment door. My mom took his suit to the cleaners every morning because he could not afford to buy another one. He would tell me stories of how he would do $1,200 a week in sales, about $60,000 that first year, which wasn't much, but he never gave up. He always strived to do better and give his guests something they had never tasted before. Over the years, and many remodelings later, he began to add new dishes to his menu, including Scampi alla Livornese, Capellini d'Angelo, and Veal Limonata Dore. He treasured these dishes and would teach only his chef, Manuel

My mother and father, Josephine and Jasper, Sr.

Cervantes, the recipes. Many restaurants have tried to copy these dishes, but only Jasper had the original recipe for our signature dishes that are still on the menu today.

Business began to grow in the 1960s, and my parents began to live their dream, purchasing the original Jasper's building and expanding the restaurant. Finally, in 1972, *Holiday* magazine honored Jasper's as one of the top 100 restaurants in America. Mobil 4 Stars, Cartier Gold Plate, AAA 4 Diamonds, and many other awards soon followed, as did rave reviews in the *Kansas City Star, Gourmet* magazine, and *Bon Appétit.* My mother and father started traveling, going to New York, San Francisco, Rome, Florence, Milan, and Paris, always bringing back new recipes and more ideas. He added new dining rooms with Murano glass chandeliers from Venice, Fortuny fabrics from Milan, Axminster carpets from England, along with fine white tablecloths, fine china, and tuxedoed waiters.

Jasper's was "the place to dine in Kansas City," as *Time* magazine reported in 1976 during the Republican National Convention. There wasn't a night in the dining room that you would not find my father making his famous Caesar Salad, tossing Pasta Carbonara, or flaming a Kansas City Peppered Steak tableside. Guests could even enjoy Crêpes Gran Vefour or Cherries Jubilee flamed at the table.

Things pretty much stayed the same at Jasper's, with my dad running the business, until my brother Leonard joined him in 1975, after my grandfather passed away. Leonard began to run the daily operations, and in 1984 I joined him and my father full-time. We opened a small Italian market named Marco Polo's. An authentic trattoria followed, Trattoria Marco Polo, as did an old-world coffee shop, Il Caffe. We worked together for thirteen years, constantly updating our menu, adding more wines, creating new dishes, and offering the Midwest a world-class operation.

In 1977, after many months of negotiations, we sold the property and buildings that we had purchased over the years at 75th Street and Wornall to a drugstore. We established our offices at 103rd Street and State Line, in the Watts Mill Shopping Center. We began to build our new Jasper's location, a casual yet elegant Italian restaurant and a unique Italian market and deli, the new Marco Polo's. Our new restaurant had been under construction for fifteen months when my father passed away. Gone was one of the most noted restaurateurs in the country, as was an era in Kansas City. It was time for Leonard and me to carry on the tradition. Sixty days later, we opened the new Jasper's Italian Restaurant and Marco Polo's Deli to rave reviews and large crowds. Customers had eagerly waited for nearly eighteen months for us to reopen.

FOOD: THE CENTER OF EVERYTHING IN OUR LIFE

People often ask me, "How old were you when you started cooking?" I remember when I was three years old helping (or pestering) my mom and nana in the family kitchen on Sundays. Food was the center of everything in our life. As a child, it was so interesting to open a refrigerator, put ingredients in a bowl, and soon after taste your creation. I can remember Nana making her famous rum cake, boiling oranges and lemons in the simple syrup and rum that would later soak into the fresh-baked sponge cake. I can still see the *babbaluci* (fresh snails) crawling out of the pot when she made her special dinner for family visiting from Sicily. I watched with excitement when my mom filled 150 cream puffs for a holiday dessert or rolled 75 to 100 meatballs for our Sunday dinners.

Nothing influenced me more than the first time I walked into my father's kitchen on 75th Street. Everything looked so big—the stoves, the ovens, even the plates. While most kids were out playing T-ball in the summer, I was sitting on the big chopping block in Jasper's kitchen and watching the cooks prepare lunch orders. My dad's chef, Manuel, always let me stir something, whether it was cannoli filling (which

Jasper, Sr. and cousin Jasper Mirabile in Sicily

Papa Leonardo and friends hunting circa 1960

I should have been folding) or custard. I spent hours making mental notes, observing the cooks making sauces, reducing stocks, grilling meats, pounding out veal, and sautéing vegetables. I was too young to work at night, so I would go home and play with my friends, but I always called my dad to ask what he was doing or what he was eating and ended every conversation with "Are you going to be late? Can I work Saturday night with my brothers?" At age 8, I finally got my first chance to work, following in my three

older brothers' footsteps by cutting the bread. My first real job was to slice the bread and prepare baskets for the bus help to take to the guests' tables. That was too easy, and I lasted about a month. I wanted to work the salad station.

As fate and luck would have it, one salad lady was sick one night, and I was allowed to help the other salad lady. I loved it—it was a dream come true! I did the salad job every Friday and Saturday night for about a year. I learned how to chop onions and cucumbers and slice tomatoes, mushrooms, and carrots. I cut the lettuce and tore the romaine, picked the spinach, and learned how to make croutons. I learned every salad dressing recipe and even added my own two cents, adjusting the Italian Dressing with more sugar and adding more Romano cheese to the Creamy Italian Dressing.

In those days, there was a small window between the kitchen and my dad's office so we could constantly communicate. On Saturdays he "worked the wheel," calling in orders to the cooks and setting up carts going out to the dining room, yet all the while keeping a watchful eye on me. He would tell his cooks, "Teach Jay how to make the tomato sauce today," or "Show Jay how I want that plate to look." I decided that someday I would be a chef, creating dishes and making people happy. As I grew older, around age 9 or 10, I began to work on the appetizer station, making dishes of Scampi alla Livornese, a recipe I have treasured and kept a secret to this day.

When I was twelve, I began to watch the "big

cooks" sauté veal, chicken, and seafood. I learned to trim whole tenderloin of beef, cut racks of lamb, and break down a whole leg of veal. I also learned the trick of boning fresh fish and shucking oysters, clams, and mussels. I began my first real on-the-line training when I was in the eighth grade, at age 14. I pleaded with my dad to make me a busboy because I wanted to wear a tuxedo. My mom and I put one together from my brothers' hand-me-downs. On my first night, I was all dressed and ready to work, and Roy, the maître d', gave me my first black bow tie. I was officially a busboy!

The wedding of Josephine and Leonardo Mirabile

I really liked it out front at first, cleaning tables, getting bread and butter and water, and just running through the dining room cleaning ashtrays and picking up dirty plates, assisting the waiters and captains. That was when I found my fondness for talking to customers and meeting celebrities, from sports personalities to owners of large corporations, as well as actors and actresses. I was enthralled by our dessert cart, which was shown to every table as the servers described each house-made dessert. I wanted to show the cart myself, so I followed our head captain one evening, making notes of his descriptions to the customers. I then went one step further, asking the pastry chef for inside information about how he made the desserts so special. Soon I was ready to show the cart. My first time, I showed it to a party of six, describing it in detail, and then added my own touch. "The chocolate cake is very good," I said. "It's my mother's recipe." I sold it to all six people!

A few months later, Robert Lawrence Balzer, noted Los Angeles restaurant critic and founder of the Travel Holiday Award, published

Cousin Reno making his famous granita (see page 142)

a cookbook. In a feature article written about Jasper's, Mr. Balzer spoke of Jasper's youngest son, Jasper, Jr., who had shown the dessert cart. Mr. Balzer was so impressed by the dessert cart that he wanted one of each. Who knew that on that first evening I was waiting on that distinguished gentleman? Because of this event, the dessert cart is still shown to every guest in our dining room today.

The year I learned to show the dessert cart, my parents took me to Italy for the first time. What a vacation! We dined in the finest restaurants in Rome, Milan, Florence, Naples, Sorrento, Calabria, and finally we spent a week with my grandfather in his hometown of Gibellina, Sicily. What a joy it was to eat with cousins I had just met for the first time, discovering dishes and foods such as Sicilian blood oranges, arancini, pasta con sarde, my cousins' gelato and granita. We also shopped at the famous Vucciria, Palermo's outdoor market. I followed my father's lead and took notes on every dish I experienced, describing presentation and taste. Remembering what my father taught me, I continue this exercise to this very day, recording everything when dining outside of Kansas City and seeking new dishes, wines, and food products to bring back to my restaurant.

Every summer during my high school years I traveled to Italy, touring wineries with their famous owners and dining at restaurants where I was greeted with open arms, as a family member returning home after a long journey. One summer I attended cooking classes in Paris, Florence, and Venice. I continued to fill notepads with ideas for creating dishes for the restaurant and the cooking classes that I teach.

The first cooking class I taught was in 1983 at the old Wolferman's Grocery Store in Fairway, Kansas. Linda Davis gave me an opportunity to showcase my father's restaurant and my cooking talent. In the first class I demonstrated Caesar Salad, Fettuccine Alfredo, Veal Limonata, and Cannoli Gelato. In 1984, I began teaching classes at our own restaurant. We had a regular attendance of forty-five to fifty people every two weeks for 14 years. I taught friends, family, and customers how to make our regional Italian dishes.

Our restaurant and market now seat 300 guests and offer diners a patio view of Indian Creek throughout all four seasons. Our menu includes old-world dishes and more contemporary plates of pasta, veal, chicken, seafood, and chops. Enoteca da Jasper features an authentic Italian wine bar and cellar room with more than 400 different wines. Marco Polo's deli, market, and pizzeria, located in the front of our restaurant, offers our famous grilled Italian sausages. We employ more than fifty people who are dedicated to cooking, serving, and satisfying the thousands of guests who dine at Jasper's.

I devour every food publication I come across; I have collected more than 2,500 cookbooks that I continuously use for research and cooking at home. I make regular trips to Italy, sometimes twice a year, visiting different regions and attending cooking classes. Each time I visit I fall in love all over again with the atmosphere, the culture, the food, and the people. This is my heritage—my love of fine foods passed down through the generations that culminate in the great Italian food and memorable experiences at Jasper's.

NEVER ON SUNDAY

My papa had our grandfather working with him. He didn't have any brothers or sisters. Growing up, I never saw my father except on Sundays. That's why today we keep our restaurant closed on Sundays. It's a Jasper's tradition and a respectful tribute to our father. It's a promise that we made to our dad before he passed away. We promised that we brothers would always work together in some fashion and that the restaurant would keep going. That was our father's dream, so after the old location closed we opened a new location at 103rd and State Line Road.

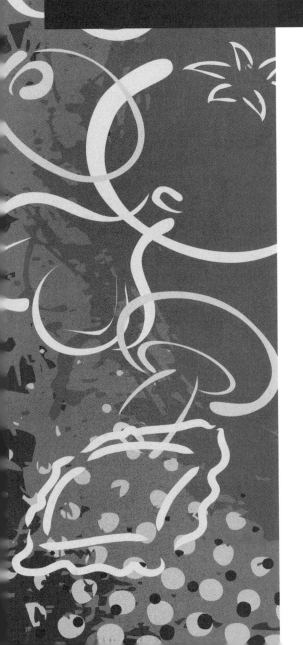

CHAPTER 2

ANTIPASTI

My family in Sicily calls the starter that begins every Italian meal grape 'u pitittu, *which means "mouth openers."* This could be small plates of olives, salami, prosciutto, assorted cheeses, or a variety of cold vegetables simply dressed with olive oil.

Personally, I always judge a restaurant or chef by the antipasti, as it gives me a preview of the dishes to come. When I plan a menu for customers or personal friends and family, I always try to serve something exciting to start the dinner. Many times I can make a meal just with antipasti, a loaf of bread, and some prosecco.

A true Italian table contains many plates of antipasti, encouraging guests to share and enjoy. So, sit down, pour a nice glass of wine, talk with family and friends, and enjoy the antipasti that will set the stage for the delicious food to follow!

GRISSINI (HOMEMADE BREADSTICKS)

SERVES 12

These thin breadsticks are fantastic. My friend Roberto Donna, chef-owner of Galileo in Washington, D.C., shared this recipe with me. The *biga* (starter) is easy to prepare, and I use it in other bread recipes.

STARTER

2 TEASPOONS ACTIVE DRY YEAST

½ CUP WARM WATER (110°F)

2½ CUPS WATER, AT ROOM TEMPERATURE

2 CUPS BREAD FLOUR

DOUGH

2 TEASPOONS ACTIVE DRY YEAST

1¾ CUPS WARM WATER (110°F)

1 CUP STARTER

6 CUPS SEMOLINA FLOUR

1 TEASPOON OLIVE OIL

1 TEASPOON SALT

To make the starter, mix the yeast and warm water together in a large bowl and let rest for 10 minutes, until foamy. Add the 2½ cups water and the bread flour and mix for 5 minutes. This mixture will be very wet. Cover loosely with a clean kitchen towel and let rise for 24 hours.

Preheat the oven to 450°F.

To make the dough, mix the yeast with the 1¾ cups warm water in a large bowl and let rest for about 10 minutes, until foamy. Scoop out 1 cup of the starter and add it to the yeast mixture, the semolina flour, olive oil, and salt. Let rest for 30 minutes.

Divide the dough into 2-inch pieces and roll each piece to form a thin breadstick.

Arrange the breadsticks ½ inch apart on a parchment-lined baking sheet and bake for 7 to 8 minutes, or until golden brown. Allow the breadsticks to cool before serving.

Tuscan Farm Bread

Makes 2 (8-inch) round loaves

Bread is central to our culture, and its unique characteristics are essential to our cuisine. This bread is rough and grainy; the crust is thick and chewy. It's served with nearly every meal in Tuscany. You'll need to allow the starter to ferment for about 12 hours, and the bread takes 6 hours of total rising time, but when the wonderful smell fills your house, and you taste this delicious loaf, you'll know it is well worth the wait.

STARTER

- 1 CUP ALL-PURPOSE FLOUR
- 1 CUP WARM WATER
- 1 TEASPOON ACTIVE DRY YEAST

DOUGH

- 1 RECIPE STARTER
- 6 CUPS ALL-PURPOSE FLOUR
- 1 CUP WHOLE WHEAT FLOUR
- 2¼ CUPS WARM WATER
- 4½ TEASPOONS SALT

To make the starter: In a large bowl, mix the flour, water, and yeast. Cover with a clean kitchen towel and let stand for 12 hours.

Preheat the oven to 430°F.

To the starter (you'll need all of it), add the flours, water, and salt. Mix for about 10 minutes. Cover loosely with a clean kitchen towel and allow to rise for 3 hours or until doubled.

Shape the dough into 18 rolls or 2 rounds and place on baking sheets, leaving 3 inches between the rolls and 6 inches between the round loaves. Allow the dough to rise for about 3 hours. Slash the top of the dough with a knife and bake for 40 minutes or until the dough is browned and crisp. Cool for at least 1 hour before slicing.

AÏOLI

MAKES 1 ¼ CUPS

This sauce, pronounced "i-OH-lee," is made of garlic and olive oil and makes a great dipping sauce for all types of bread. The key to success with aïoli is to work very slowly and keep your ingredients and cooking tools at room temperature.

2 TO 3 CLOVES GARLIC, CHOPPED

COARSE SEA OR KOSHER SALT AND
    FRESHLY GROUND BLACK PEPPER

1 EGG YOLK, AT ROOM TEMPERATURE

JUICE OF ½ LEMON

⅔ CUP OLIVE OIL (*NOT* EXTRA VIRGIN)

⅓ CUP EXTRA VIRGIN OLIVE OIL

In a food processor or a blender, combine the garlic and a large pinch of salt and pulse for 2 seconds. Add the egg yolk and lemon juice, pulse until blended, and then turn the speed to low and begin adding the olive oil slowly, in a thin stream, first the pure olive oil and then the extra virgin. If the sauce becomes too thick, thin it out with some room-temperature water and continue adding oil until you've used all of it. Finish with pepper and a bit more salt to taste.

CHARRED RAPINI, WISCONSIN BURRATA, AND CRISPY CIABATTA

SERVES 4

Burrata is a fresh Italian cheese made from mozzarella and cream. The name *burrata* means "buttered" in Italian. Ciabatta (ch'yah-BAH-tah) means "slipper" in Italian, referring to the bread's shape. Rapini, also known as *broccoli rabe,* is commonly featured in Italian and Chinese dishes. This is a very simple starter recipe that complements any meal.

2 BUNCHES RAPINI (ABOUT 1 POUND)

EXTRA VIRGIN OLIVE OIL

4 THICK SLICES CIABATTA

1 POUND WISCONSIN BURRATA

HOT RED PEPPER FLAKES, FOR SERVING

SICILIAN SEA SALT, FOR SERVING

Prepare a charcoal grill.

Clean the rapini and trim about 1 inch off the stem ends. In a medium saucepan, bring 8 cups of water to a boil. Cook the rapini in the boiling water for about 5 minutes. Drain and set aside.

Brush the rapini with the olive oil and place it on the grill. Cook until charred on both sides, 3 to 5 minutes, turning as needed. Remove the rapini from the grill and place it in the refrigerator to chill while you prepare the remaining ingredients.

Toast the slices of ciabatta on both sides on the grill until crispy and arrange them on a chilled serving platter. Arrange some of the rapini and some of the burrata side by side on top of each slice of bread. Drizzle with extra virgin olive oil and sprinkle with red pepper flakes and sea salt.

CIABATTA CON PROSCIUTTO DI PARMA FORMAGGIO

SERVES 3 TO 4

This savory antipasto is a great "pass around" dish for an informal gathering. The melted cheese and prosciutto on crispy bread is just like an open-faced grilled cheese sandwich!

½ CUP EXTRA VIRGIN OLIVE OIL

1 CUP SLICED MUSHROOMS (ABOUT 3 OUNCES)

3 TO 4 CANNED ARTICHOKE HEARTS

2 TO 3 CLOVES GARLIC

¼ CUP CHOPPED ITALIAN PARSLEY

8 SLICES PROSCIUTTO DI PARMA

8 SLICES CIABATTA, BRUSHED WITH OLIVE OIL AND GRILLED OR BROILED UNTIL CRISP

GRATED PARMIGIANO-REGGIANO CHEESE, FOR SERVING

Heat the olive oil in a large sauté pan over medium heat. Add the mushrooms and artichoke hearts and sauté for 3 to 4 minutes. Add the garlic and parsley and sauté for 3 to 4 minutes longer. Transfer the mixture to a bowl and set aside.

In the oil remaining in the pan, sauté the prosciutto slices for 2 to 3 minutes, until warmed and slightly crisp.

To serve, lay a slice of prosciutto on the grilled ciabatta, top with some of the mushroom and artichoke mixture, and sprinkle with the grated cheese.

HEIRLOOM TOMATO BRUSCHETTA

SERVES 4

I absolutely love heirloom tomatoes! I love them for their variety of shapes, colors, textures, and flavors. Some say that the seeds for cultivating heirloom tomatoes might be more than 100 years old.

HEIRLOOM TOMATO MIXTURE

- 2 HEIRLOOM TOMATOES, CORED, SEEDED, AND DICED
- ¼ CUP MINCED ONION
- 1 CLOVE GARLIC, FINELY CHOPPED
- ¼ CUP EXTRA VIRGIN OLIVE OIL
- 1 TABLESPOON BALSAMIC VINEGAR
- 1 SCALLION, CHOPPED
- 1 TABLESPOON CHOPPED CHIVES

BRUSCHETTA

- 1 CLOVE GARLIC, CRUSHED
- 4 SLICES CIABATTA, ½ INCH THICK
- OLIVE OIL, FOR BRUSHING
- SALT
- MINCED CHIVES, FOR GARNISH

To make the heirloom tomato mixture, combine the tomatoes, onion, garlic, olive oil, vinegar, scallion, and chives. Mix well and set aside for up to 4 hours.

Preheat the broiler.

Lightly rub the garlic on the ciabatta slices, brush them with olive oil, and broil until slightly browned. Season with salt to taste. Top the crispy bread with the heirloom tomato mixture. Garnish with chives and serve.

Peperonata Siciliano

SERVES 4 TO 6

This classic Sicilian *agrodolce,* or sour-and-sweet dish, is always served on an antipasto tray. I prefer to serve it chilled with crispy crackers, crostini, or as an accompaniment to fried pork chops.

6 ASSORTED BELL PEPPERS, RED, GREEN, AND YELLOW

2 TO 3 TABLESPOONS OLIVE OIL

1 MEDIUM ONION, CHOPPED

3 CLOVES GARLIC, CHOPPED

1½ POUNDS CHERRY TOMATOES, HALVED

SALT AND FRESHLY GROUND BLACK PEPPER

2 SPRIGS BASIL

1 TABLESPOON BALSAMIC VINEGAR (OPTIONAL)

1 TABLESPOON DRAINED CAPERS

1 TABLESPOON RAISINS

½ TEASPOON SUGAR

GENOA SALAMI, FOR SERVING

CROSTINI, FOR SERVING

Cut the peppers in half, remove the seeds and ribs, quarter the peppers, and then cut them crosswise into ½-inch strips.

Heat the olive oil in a sauté pan over medium heat and add the onion. Sauté for 5 minutes. Add the garlic and peppers and sauté for 5 more minutes. Add the tomatoes, mix well, and season with salt and pepper to taste. Add the basil sprigs and mix well. Cover the pan, reduce the heat to low, and leave to sweat for 15 minutes. This allows the flavors to seep out without overcooking or allowing the mixture to caramelize.

Stir in the vinegar, if using, and capers, then add the raisins and sugar. Cool and then serve with thin slices of salami and crostini.

POLENTA CON FUNGHI E FORMAGGIO

SERVES 4 TO 6

When my family first opened our trattoria on 75th Street, we were the first to offer polenta, which has a very creamy consistency. I didn't want to serve it plain, so I decided to create a sauce that would complement the polenta. The combination of Marsala and Gorgonzola works well, and I often serve this in the winter as an accompaniment to chicken, short ribs, or osso buco.

POLENTA

- 4 CUPS CHICKEN STOCK
- 1 CUP STONE-GROUND ITALIAN CORNMEAL
- 2 TABLESPOONS BUTTER
- 8 OUNCES FONTINA CHEESE, GRATED (ABOUT 2 CUPS)
- ½ CUP HEAVY CREAM
- SALT AND FRESHLY GROUND BLACK PEPPER

GORGONZOLA AND MUSHROOM SAUCE

- 1 TABLESPOON BUTTER
- 8 MEDIUM WHITE BUTTON MUSHROOMS, THINLY SLICED
- ¼ CUP MARSALA
- 2 CUPS HEAVY CREAM
- ½ CUP CRUMBLED GORGONZOLA CHEESE (ABOUT 2 OUNCES)
- 1 TO 2 SPRIGS ROSEMARY, FOR GARNISH

To make the polenta, bring the chicken stock to a boil in a 3-quart pot. Stir in the cornmeal and cook for 5 to 6 minutes, stirring constantly. Whisk in the butter, cheese, and cream. Season with salt and pepper to taste.

To make the sauce, melt the butter in a medium skillet. Add the mushrooms and sauté over medium heat for 2 to 3 minutes, until soft. Add the Marsala and cook for about 4 minutes, until the liquid is reduced. Add the cream and whisk in the Gorgonzola. Serve over the polenta. Top each serving with some rosemary and serve.

Arancini (Sicilian Rice Balls)

Makes about 30 rice balls

Imagine spending a day in the city of Palermo, a market city for well over 3,000 years. You find yourself in Vucciria, one of the oldest and most famous markets in Palermo. It's teeming with activity, people, dogs, cats, loud talking. It's a feast for the senses! Sit and enjoy, and have a little something to eat, such as one of my favorite dishes—arancini. *Arancini* means "little oranges," and that is what they look like when cooked. This dish is usually reserved for holidays but can be enjoyed anytime. Be sure to serve this with a little side dish of *sugo,* or "sauce."

1 POUND WHITE RICE (ABOUT 2½ CUPS)

4 EGGS

½ CUP GRATED CHEESE, SUCH AS ROMANO OR PARMESAN

SALT AND FRESHLY GROUND BLACK PEPPER

1 MEDIUM ONION, CHOPPED

1½ POUNDS GROUND BEEF OR BULK ITALIAN SAUSAGE

1 CUP PLUS 2 TABLESPOONS OLIVE OIL

½ (6-OUNCE) CAN TOMATO PASTE, MIXED WITH 3 TABLESPOONS WATER

3 CUPS EXTRA-FINE BREAD CRUMBS

Cook the rice according to the package directions until tender. Drain and let cool slightly. Add two of the eggs, the cheese, and salt and pepper to taste. Mix well and set aside.

While the rice is cooking, brown the onion and ground beef in 2 tablespoons of the olive oil. Add the tomato paste and simmer for a few minutes. Season with salt and pepper. Let cool.

Place 2 tablespoons of cooked rice in the palm of your hand. Make a well in the rice and place about 1 tablespoon of the meat mixture in the well. Mold the rice around the meat to form a ball or egg shape. Repeat with the remaining rice and meat.

Heat the remaining cup of olive oil in a sauté pan over high heat. Beat the remaining 2 eggs in a bowl. Dip the rice balls in the beaten eggs, roll them in the bread crumbs, and drop them in the hot oil, making sure they're not touching one another. Sauté the arancini until they're golden brown on all sides, about 3 minutes. Use a slotted spoon to remove the arancini from the oil and drain them on paper towels. Repeat with any remaining arancini. Serve warm.

EGGPLANT OTHELLO

SERVES 4

The eggplant came to Sicily from the Middle East in the early Middle Ages. It's a spongy, mild-tasting vegetable that comes in many shapes, colors, and sizes. It's meaty yet low in calories. Be sure to leave the skin of the eggplant intact to hold the tender slices together. To make this a vegetarian dish, omit the Italian sausage.

1 LARGE EGGPLANT, CUT LENGTHWISE INTO 6 TO 8 SLICES

SALT

1 CUP OLIVE OIL

4 OUNCES BULK ITALIAN SAUSAGE

8 OUNCES RICOTTA CHEESE (1 CUP)

1 TABLESPOON CHOPPED ITALIAN PARSLEY

2 EGGS, BEATEN

2 OUNCES PARMIGIANO-REGGIANO CHEESE, GRATED (ABOUT ½ CUP)

1½ CUPS TOMATO SAUCE

4 SLICES PROVOLONE CHEESE, CUT INTO STRIPS

Preheat the oven to 400°F. Place the eggplant slices on a baking sheet, lightly salt them, and let them sit for about 30 minutes to sweat. Rinse them and pat them dry.

Heat the olive oil in a large skillet over medium-high heat. Salt the eggplant slices and sauté on both sides for 4 to 5 minutes, until the slices are soft and golden in color. Transfer the eggplant from the skillet to paper towels and pat with a paper towel to absorb excess oil.

Place the sausage in the same skillet and cook thoroughly, about 20 minutes. Drain off any excess fat.

In a large mixing bowl, blend the ricotta cheese, parsley, eggs, and Parmesan. Add the cooked sausage to the cheese mixture and blend together.

Place 2 to 3 tablespoons of the mixture on each eggplant slice and roll up. Place in a baking dish, seam side down, cover with tomato sauce, and bake for 10 minutes. Turn the oven to broil.

Remove the baking dish from the oven and place strips of provolone cheese on top of each eggplant roll. Broil for 30 to 45 seconds, or until the cheese melts. Serve hot.

Artichoke Bambolinis

Serves 6

This is traditional Sicilian street food at its finest. I first had these in the famous Palermo Market, the Vucciria. I like to serve this unique dish at private parties.

1 CUP BOILING WATER

1 CUP ALL-PURPOSE FLOUR

SALT

1 HEAPING TABLESPOON SOLID
VEGETABLE SHORTENING

3 EGGS

1 CUP DICED, DRAINED, CANNED
ARTICHOKE HEARTS

VEGETABLE OR OLIVE OIL, FOR FRYING

Bring the water to a boil in a 2-quart pot. Remove from the heat and add the flour, a dash of salt, and the shortening. Beat well with a fork. Beat in the eggs, one at a time. Fold in the artichoke hearts.

Fill a sauté pan with 1 inch of oil and heat to 375°F on a deep-frying thermometer. Spoon rounded tablespoons of the mixture into the hot oil and cook for about 5 minutes, or until golden brown on all sides, turning as needed. Remove from the pan and drain on paper towels. Season with salt and serve.

PEPPERS ANGELO

SERVES 6 TO 12

The first restaurant that I dined in while visiting New York City was Angelo's on Mulberry Street. Ironically, this is the first New York restaurant my father was taken to by my grandfather. I love the stuffed peppers, the linguine with fresh clams, and all the veal dishes at Angelo's. My father worked on this recipe many times, adding anchovies, fewer croutons, and tomatoes until he was satisfied with the dish. Whenever I visit New York as a guest chef or for pleasure, I always head straight down to Little Italy at Mulberry and Grand and enjoy my dinner at Angelo's.

¼ CUP OLIVE OIL

1 LARGE EGGPLANT, CUBED

½ MEDIUM ONION, CUT INTO VERY THIN STRIPS

1 (15-OUNCE) CAN TOMATOES, CHOPPED

3 CLOVES GARLIC, CHOPPED

¼ TEASPOON DRIED BASIL

½ TEASPOON SUGAR

½ TEASPOON SALT

FRESHLY GROUND BLACK PEPPER

4 ANCHOVIES, CHOPPED

18 BLACK OLIVES, PITTED AND HALVED

5 LARGE MUSHROOMS, SLICED

3 TABLESPOONS DRAINED CAPERS

3 CUPS PLAIN CROUTONS

2 TABLESPOONS CREAM SHERRY

¼ CUP RAISINS

6 GREEN BELL PEPPERS, HALVED AND BOILED FOR 10 MINUTES

2 CUPS HOT JASPER'S CLASSIC MARINARA (PAGE 59), FOR SERVING

Preheat the oven to 350°F.

Heat the olive oil in a sauté pan over medium heat, add the eggplant and onion, and sauté for about 7 minutes, until soft. Add the tomatoes, garlic, basil, sugar, salt, and pepper to taste. Continue to sauté until the onion is translucent, 3 to 4 minutes longer. Stir in the anchovies and olives. Cook for about 5 minutes, then add the mushrooms and capers.

Raise the heat to medium-high and sauté for 2 to 3 minutes. Add the croutons and stir well. Add the sherry and cook, stirring, until the croutons soak up all of the sauce, about 3 minutes. Add the raisins and mix well.

Stuff the mixture into each half pepper. Place the peppers on a baking sheet and roast for 35 minutes, or until the peppers are tender. Be sure not to overcook the peppers or they will get mushy.

Top each pepper with hot marinara sauce and serve.

SICILIAN FRITTATA

SERVES 6 TO 8

No true Sicilian meal is complete without a frittata. In the spring I use fresh asparagus, lightly boiled. In the winter I may use fried potatoes, peppers, and onions. I even use cauliflower and broccoli. At the restaurant I serve this at lunch as some restaurants would an omelet. Serve this on a beautiful round platter and cut it into wedges, like a pie, or as a centerpiece on your buffet.

¼ CUP OLIVE OIL

1 BUNCH SCALLIONS, CHOPPED

8 OUNCES FROZEN ARTICHOKE HEARTS, THAWED

12 EGGS

¼ CUP MILK

1 TABLESPOON CHOPPED ITALIAN PARSLEY

8 OUNCES MOZZARELLA CHEESE, SHREDDED (ABOUT 2 CUPS)

DASH OF DRIED BASIL

¼ TEASPOON SALT

¼ TEASPOON FRESHLY GROUND BLACK PEPPER

Preheat the oven to 325°F.

Heat the olive oil in a 10- to 12-inch ovenproof skillet, add the scallions and artichoke hearts, and cook over medium-high heat until golden, 4 to 5 minutes. In a large mixing bowl, beat the eggs until frothy. Add the milk and beat again. Stir in the parsley, mozzarella, basil, salt, and pepper. Add the egg mixture to the artichoke mixture and mix well. Bake for 15 minutes, or until firm. Slice and serve warm.

JASPER'S CARPACCIO

SERVES 8

I served this dish to rave reviews at the James Beard House in 1995, and it has since become a permanent dish on my menu. It's always included at my receptions or antipasto hour, and I like to serve it with Pinot Grigio or prosecco. Crostini, a Tuscan specialty, are slices of toast that are thinner than bruschetta and are usually brushed with olive oil. Always be sure to offer cracked black pepper, which was once a precious twelfth-century commodity controlled by the Venetians and used as currency in Europe.

1 POUND SMOKED SALMON, OR RAW KANSAS CITY STRIP OR FILET MIGNON, SLICED PAPER-THIN

2 EGG YOLKS

1 ½ TEASPOONS DIJON MUSTARD

2 TABLESPOONS FRESHLY SQUEEZED LEMON JUICE

1 SHALLOT, MINCED

1 TABLESPOON MINCED FRESH TARRAGON

½ CUP EXTRA VIRGIN OLIVE OIL

SALT AND FRESHLY GROUND BLACK PEPPER

DRAINED CAPERS, FOR GARNISH

CROSTINI, FOR SERVING

Place the sliced salmon or beef on a chilled plate.

Whisk the egg yolks in a large mixing bowl. Add the mustard, lemon juice, shallot, and tarragon. Blend well. Add the olive oil in a thin stream, whisking until the sauce thickens. Add salt and pepper to taste.

Drizzle the sauce over the carpaccio and garnish with the capers. Offer your guests freshly cracked black pepper and serve with crostini.

PEPERONI DON SALVATORE

SERVES 4

This is a recipe I discovered in Venice during my cooking school summer at the Gritti Palace, which was built in 1525. The chef told me that Ernest Hemingway was a regular at the palace and this was his favorite dish. We served this dish back in the late seventies, and I have since added it back to my menu.

8 OUNCES ITALIAN CANNED TUNA

6 ANCHOVY FILLETS

1 CUP OLIVE OIL

10 CAPERS, DRAINED

4 CORNICHONS, DRAINED

JUICE OF 2 LEMONS

8 OUNCES FRESH ITALIAN GOAT CHEESE

4 ROASTED RED BELL PEPPERS, SEEDED AND CUT LENGTHWISE INTO 4 PIECES EACH

FRESHLY CRACKED BLACK PEPPER, FOR GARNISH

Put the tuna, anchovies, olive oil, capers, cornichons, and lemon juice in a blender and blend for 1 minute. Add the goat cheese and blend until smooth. Place 1 to 2 teaspoons of the tuna mixture on each piece of roasted pepper. Garnish with cracked pepper.

What Is a Restaurant?

Presented to my father, Jasper, Sr., by his son James

Somewhere between the excitement of the Broadway stage and a September football scrimmage, we find the extraordinary phenomenon called THE RESTAURANT. Restaurants come in assorted sizes, prices, and themes, but all restaurants have the same creed: serve people every minute of every hour of every day.

Restaurants are a composite. They are there to fill up, flake out, celebrate, and remember. Even to forget. To your competition, you are always filled, you are the greatest chef, have the cleanest kitchen, and have the best wine list. To your guest, you are a swinger, a party boy, living the life of Riley. And someday, as they always say, "When I retire, I am going to open a place of my own."

Restaurants live with phrases like "We're two dishwashers short," "The waiter didn't show," "The cook quit," and "What is the count?"

Your customer of 10 years just told you his veal was tough, and this is the last time you'll see him.

It's the only business where you are only as good as your last meal.

A restaurant is a smile on your face with two waiters short; a new tux with tomato sauce on the sleeve; and shaking hands with the owner of the Kansas City Chiefs, while your left hand is on the plunger. It's smiling at strangers with only a few hours of sleep, while your sons ask, "When is Dad coming home?" It's having one son as a lawyer, and one as a doc, two in the business and a wife on the time clock.

A restaurant is trying to be Cecil B. DeMille and Rodgers and Hart, while the script is written by the bank. It takes the finesse of an art collector with the fortitude and skill of a plumber. It is 5:00 p.m., and the sauces are checked, the cooks are late, the bartender quit, and the show must go on, so you gather your wits, your back has finally broken, but the curtain has risen.

The bank just called at 5:30 p.m. The deposit got lost, and the accounts are overdrawn, and you holler at the accountant as he screws up the costs, but by now it's 6:00 p.m. and the show begins.

A restaurant is the Super Bowl, the World Series, and Oscar night all rolled into one when you hear, "It's the best meal I've had, and we'll be back!"

Thanks, Dad, for being the director and for teaching us what a restaurant is.

Papa Mirabile's Lumache

SERVES 4

This is one of our oldest recipes, although it's not usually found on Italian menus. When I see young people order this dish, it takes me back to my childhood, when I was always trying something different at a nice restaurant. This makes more garlic butter than you'll need for the recipe. Reserve the extra and use it on toast or as a seasoning butter for steaks or seafood.

1 SHALLOT, FINELY CHOPPED

½ CUP CHOPPED ITALIAN PARSLEY

6 CLOVES GARLIC, MINCED

4 TABLESPOONS (½ STICK) BUTTER

1 ½ TEASPOONS SALT

¼ TEASPOON FRESHLY GROUND
   BLACK PEPPER

6 TO 8 ASSORTED MUSHROOMS, THINLY SLICED

24 ESCARGOTS, DRAINED, RINSED,
   AND PATTED DRY

2 OUNCES WHITE WINE

4 SLICES GARLIC TOAST

In a bowl, combine the shallot, parsley, garlic, butter, salt, and pepper. Mix well and chill for about 10 minutes.

Heat the chilled butter mixture in a large sauté pan over medium heat. Add the mushrooms and escargots. Sauté for 4 to 5 minutes. Splash the pan with the wine and serve over freshly toasted garlic bread.

FOCACCIA CRAB CAKES

SERVES 6

This is a new twist on an all-time favorite appetizer that's guaranteed to please all of your senses. When I had the privilege of being invited to cook at the James Beard House in New York City, I had to showcase my restaurant by offering something different and exciting. Crab cakes are always popular as an appetizer, but I added a special flair to the recipe that completely changed the texture and gave them outstanding flavor but kept them very light! I simply used focaccia in place of regular bread crumbs. I served them on a bed of chilled rémoulade sauce with roasted peppers and extra virgin olive oil. Be sure to also try my Chilled Seafood Sauce, which follows this recipe.

ROASTED RED PEPPER SAUCE

- 1 CUP ROASTED RED PEPPERS
- ¼ CUP MINCED ONION
- 1 CUP DICED GREEN BELL PEPPER
- 18 TO 20 CAPERS, DRAINED
- 1 CUP MAYONNAISE
- 2 TABLESPOONS FRESHLY SQUEEZED LEMON JUICE
- ½ TEASPOON HOT SAUCE
- SALT

CRAB CAKES

- ¼ CUP OLIVE OIL, FOR SAUTÉING
- ½ MEDIUM WHITE ONION, MINCED
- 1 STALK CELERY, DICED
- ½ CUP MINCED GREEN BELL PEPPER
- 1 WHOLE ROASTED PEPPER, DICED
- 1 POUND CRABMEAT
- 2 CUPS FOCACCIA CRUMBS
- 2 TEASPOONS WORCESTERSHIRE SAUCE
- 1½ TEASPOONS HOT SAUCE
- 1 TEASPOON SALT
- 3 EGGS

To make the roasted red pepper sauce, combine the roasted red peppers, onion, green pepper, and capers in a food processor. Pulse until finely chopped. Add the mayonnaise, lemon juice, and hot sauce. Season with salt to taste. Chill until ready to serve.

To make the crab cakes, heat 1 tablespoon of the olive oil in a small skillet. Add the onion, celery, and green pepper and sauté over medium heat for 5 to 6 minutes, until soft. In a mixing bowl, combine the cooked onion, celery, and green pepper with the roasted pepper, crabmeat, focaccia crumbs, Worcestershire sauce, hot sauce, and salt and mix thoroughly.

Add the eggs, blend well, and form into 12 patties. Heat the remaining olive oil in a large skillet or sauté pan, add the crab cakes, and sauté over medium-high heat until golden brown on both sides, 6 to 8 minutes total. Serve warm topped with roasted red pepper sauce.

JASPER'S CHILLED SEAFOOD SAUCE

MAKES 3 CUPS

This sauce is always served at my home with chilled shrimp, crab, or crab cakes. At Jasper's, I sauté fresh sole with a Parmigiano crust and also serve this sauce alongside the dish.

1 MEDIUM WHITE ONION

3 STALKS CELERY

1 GREEN BELL PEPPER

1 RED BELL PEPPER OR PIMIENTO

2 CUPS MAYONNAISE

½ TEASPOON HOT RED PEPPER FLAKES

1 TEASPOON SALT

JUICE OF ½ LEMON

In a blender or food processor, combine the onion, celery, and bell peppers and blend until minced. Transfer to a mixing bowl and fold in the mayonnaise. Add the red pepper flakes, salt, and lemon juice and mix together. Serve chilled.

CLAMS OREGANATO

SERVES 4

This is a very simple but elegant appetizer. I prefer to use littleneck clams. They are the smallest of the hard-shell family and come from the coast of Long Island, New York. They are very tender and cook rather quickly. Over the years, I've shucked hundreds of clams for parties!

½ TEASPOON DRIED OREGANO

1 CUP FRESH ITALIAN BREAD CRUMBS

½ CUP GRATED ROMANO CHEESE
  (ABOUT 2 OUNCES)

4 TO 6 CLOVES GARLIC, MINCED

½ CUP FINELY CHOPPED ITALIAN PARSLEY

24 LITTLENECK CLAMS

2 TABLESPOONS EXTRA VIRGIN OLIVE OIL

¼ CUP DRY WHITE WINE (OPTIONAL)

LEMON WEDGES, FOR GARNISH

PARSLEY SPRIGS, FOR GARNISH

Place the oregano, bread crumbs, cheese, and garlic in a food processor. Pulse for 1 to 2 minutes to blend. Add the chopped parsley and mix for 30 to 45 seconds. Set aside or place in a sealed container and store in the refrigerator for up to 30 days.

Preheat the oven to 350°F.

Brush the outside of the clams to clean them. Open the clams, rinse away any sand, and cut the muscle holding the clam to the shell, keeping the clam in the shell. Place a dab of olive oil on each clam and cover each clam with an ample amount of the bread crumb mixture. Place the clams in a large baking pan. To add flavor to the finished dish, add about ¼ cup dry white wine, if using, to the baking pan. Bake for 7 to 10 minutes, or until the bread crumb mixture is golden brown.

To serve, arrange the clams on a serving platter and surround with lemon wedges and sprigs of Italian parsley.

OYSTERS CHRISTINA

SERVES 2

Even if you don't normally like oysters, you are going to love this unique recipe. The savory taste of lemon and the crispy texture of the coating give you a reason to try oysters again. This dish is only served on the seasonal menu at Jasper's and always receives rave reviews.

½ CUP GRATED LEMON ZEST

½ CUP GRATED ROMANO CHEESE

½ CUP BREAD CRUMBS

PINCH OF SALT

PINCH OF FRESHLY GROUND WHITE PEPPER

1 EGG

6 FRESHLY SHUCKED OYSTERS

½ CUP OLIVE OIL

LEMON SLICES, FOR GARNISH

In a large mixing bowl, combine the lemon zest, cheese, bread crumbs, salt, and pepper. In a separate mixing bowl, whisk the egg. Dip the oysters into the egg and then into the bread crumb mixture.

Heat the olive oil in a large skillet over low heat, add the oysters, and sauté for about 2 minutes. Turn and cook for 1 minute. Garnish with lemon slices and serve.

Sicilian Artichokes

SERVES 4

The artichoke is one of the oldest known foods and has delighted and nourished people for several thousand years. It is a delicious vegetable that many people shy away from cooking, but don't be afraid! This is a very simple beginner's recipe. All it requires is a little trimming and stuffing, and you'll have a great appetizer or meal. Be sure to savor the artichoke heart—it's the best part! Just clean around it when you've finished eating artichoke leaves.

4 WHOLE ARTICHOKES

2 CUPS BREAD CRUMBS

4 CLOVES FRESH GARLIC, MINCED

½ CUP GRATED BELGIOIOSO ROMANO CHEESE

¼ CUP WATER

¼ CUP FINELY CHOPPED PARSLEY

½ CUP OLIVE OIL

Prepare the artichokes: Trim them flat across the top and remove the stem and the hard, dry outer leaves. Boil them in lightly salted water for 10 minutes. Remove the artichokes from the water and set them aside to cool while you prepare the stuffing.

In a mixing bowl, combine the bread crumbs, minced garlic, Romano cheese, water, parsley, and olive oil and mix well.

Preheat the oven to 325°F.

Once the artichokes have cooled enough to handle them, slightly pull each of the petals away from the center to make wells. Fill the wells with the bread-crumb mixture. Place the stuffed artichokes in a baking dish and fill with 1 cup water to steam. Drizzle with more olive oil if desired. Cover the dish with foil and bake for 30 to 45 minutes.

Serve warm.

MITH (Mirabile in the House)

We have something in our family called MITH. It stands for Mirabile in the House. In 55 years of doing business, there has never been one single time—not one single day—that this restaurant has been open that there was not a Mirabile family member in the house.

A Mirabile is always here. Even when my brother Leonard and I happen to be gone at the same time, which is almost unheard of, my brother Salvatore, who is the attorney, or my brother James, who is the doctor, covers for us.

We're very fortunate that my nephew Jasper is in the family business. We call him J3. When customers come into Jasper's, they'll always meet a member of the Mirabile family. Usually there are two or three of us here. That's what makes our restaurant unique, especially distinct from the chain restaurants. Our customers know that when they dine here the food is being checked by a family member and we are constantly looking out for our friends who come in the door. All of our customers are our friends! We want them to feel comfortable and welcome, so we want to know their names. We are here to prepare a delicious meal, served in a friendly setting that makes people want to keep coming back.

We are not just another place that serves spaghetti and meatballs; we serve excellent Italian dishes, many made from old family recipes, and we offer a wonderful dining experience!

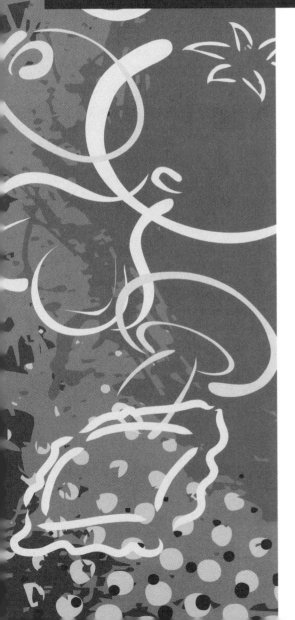

CHAPTER 3

ZUPPA E INSALATA

I *call these my in-between courses.* Some are very simple but unique. Other salads are more complex and require extra time and passion to create.

When it comes to soup, there is no better comfort dish that can actually showcase so many different ingredients. What can be better than a bowl of rewarmed soup, a loaf of crusty bread, and a glass of vino?

My motto is "Never serve a plain salad!" Dress it up, add texture and a mix of flavors, with dressings and vinaigrettes infused with spices and fruits. Surprisingly, I always spend more time with my salads than any other dish when developing recipes for my cooking classes. I want to be sure to add seasonal ingredients, make the dressings thicker with honey, and always try to bring them up to another level.

Always use vegetables in season. It's an Italian tradition.

JASPER, JR., JAMES BEARD HOUSE LOBSTER CAPPUCCINO

SERVES 6

This is the dish that opened the door for me to the James Beard House. I was one of the first chefs from Kansas City (and one of the first Italian chefs) invited to cook at the prestigious home of America's famous cookbook author and chef James Beard. The dish I created not only had to meet the standards of excellence set forth by the James Beard Foundation; it had to appeal to the New York critics as well! I started off the event with this Lobster Cappuccino, and it has become my signature dish.

2 TO 4 TABLESPOONS BUTTER

¼ CUP CHOPPED ONION

1 POUND LOBSTER MEAT, MINCED

¼ CUP CREAM SHERRY

1 TABLESPOON LOBSTER BASE

3 CUPS HEAVY CREAM

PINCH OF DRIED TARRAGON

¼ POUND PANCETTA (ITALIAN BACON), UNROLLED AND FINELY CHOPPED

FRESHLY WHIPPED CREAM, FOR TOPPING

Melt 2 tablespoons of the butter in a 2-quart pot over medium heat and sauté the onion until translucent. Add the lobster meat and continue to cook for 6 to 8 minutes.

Add the sherry, bring to a boil over medium heat, and boil until the mixture is reduced by about half. Add the lobster base, cream, and tarragon. Bring to a boil, lower the heat, and simmer slowly for about 12 minutes.

In a large pan, fry the pancetta until crispy. Wrap the fried pancetta in paper towels to absorb grease, then crumble it and set aside.

Divide the lobster mixture among 6 cappuccino or espresso cups; top each with whipped cream and crispy pancetta.

Note: You can buy lobster base at specialty food stores and online.

Tuscan Beef Stew

Serves 2 to 3

It is said that there is no such thing as "Italian food," just local cooking traditions. This recipe epitomizes Tuscan cuisine and local ingredients prepared with simplicity.

1 ½ pounds extra-lean stewing beef, cut into 1-inch cubes

2 cups Italian red wine

1 ½ teaspoons beef bouillon granules or base

4 medium Yukon Gold potatoes, peeled and cubed

3 carrots, sliced

2 medium yellow onions, cubed

1 stalk celery, sliced

1 (28-ounce) can whole San Marzano tomatoes

1 clove garlic, crushed

2 tablespoons fresh rosemary leaves

½ teaspoon cornstarch

¼ cup cold water

Place the beef, wine, bouillon, potatoes, carrots, onions, celery, tomatoes with their juices, garlic, and rosemary in a slow cooker and cook on low heat for 8 to 10 hours, until the beef is tender. Mix the cornstarch with the water and add it to the stew. Turn the slow cooker to high and stir the stew until thickened. Serve hot. It's great with Tuscan Farm Bread (page 12).

ASPARAGUS SOUP WITH CRISPY PROSCIUTTO

SERVES 4 TO 6

Asparagus is a member of the lily family, which also includes onions, garlic, leeks, turnips, and gladiolus. The ancient Greeks liked wild asparagus, and the Romans first began to cultivate it. Julius Caesar first tried it in Lombardy served with melted butter—which is the way many people still serve it. There's an old Roman saying that translates to "as quick as cooking asparagus," and this holds true for the cooking process today.

2 BUNCHES FRESH ASPARAGUS
(ABOUT 2 POUNDS)

1 MEDIUM POTATO, PEELED AND DICED

½ CUP MINCED CARROT

½ CUP MINCED SCALLION

4 CUPS CHICKEN STOCK

2 CUPS HEAVY CREAM

SALT AND FRESHLY GROUND BLACK PEPPER

½ TEASPOON BUTTER

4 OUNCES PROSCIUTTO, FINELY DICED

EXTRA VIRGIN OLIVE OIL, FOR GARNISH

1 TABLESPOON FINELY CHOPPED CHIVES,
FOR GARNISH

Prepare the asparagus by snapping off the tough part at the base and cutting the spears into pieces about 1½ inches long. Cut and save about 10 asparagus tips for garnish.

In a large saucepan, mix together the potato, carrot, scallion, and chicken stock. Bring to a boil over medium-high heat and cook for 10 minutes. Add the asparagus and simmer until the vegetables are tender, about 10 more minutes.

Remove the pan from the heat and allow the mixture to cool. Puree the cooled mixture in a blender or food processor. You may want to strain the purée to remove any fibers from the asparagus. If you want a thinner soup, add more chicken stock to achieve the desired consistency.

Mix in the cream and season with salt and pepper to taste. Chill in the refrigerator for about 3 hours.

While the soup is chilling, melt the butter in a sauté pan over medium-high heat and sauté the prosciutto until crisp. Wrap in paper towels to absorb excess grease before crumbling. Fill a small saucepan with water and bring it to a boil over medium-high heat. Blanch the asparagus tips for about 3 minutes. Drain and set aside.

Serve the soup chilled, garnished with asparagus tips, a drizzle of extra virgin olive oil, a sprinkling of chives, and crispy prosciutto crumbles.

TRADITIONAL CARABACCIA

SERVES 6 TO 8

Carabaccia, thought to be the ancestor of today's onion soup, was introduced to France by Catherine de Médicis. A rich stock is needed for this dish, and I like to lace it with a little sweet cream sherry or cognac at the end. The Tuscans would never throw bread away, and that is why it is added to this soup. I had this soup at Il Latini in Florence, where they added some cabbage for extra flavor.

8 TABLESPOONS (1 STICK) BUTTER

4 LARGE WHITE ONIONS, CHOPPED

1 TABLESPOON ALL-PURPOSE FLOUR

1 CUP CREAM SHERRY

½ TEASPOON DRIED THYME

4 CUPS BEEF STOCK

¼ CUP COGNAC OR CREAM SHERRY

SALT AND FRESHLY GROUND BLACK PEPPER

6 TO 8 THICK SLICES CIABATTA

1 CLOVE GARLIC, HALVED

6 TO 8 SLICES FONTINA CHEESE

Melt the butter in a large stockpot over medium heat. Add the onions and sauté until golden, 8 to 10 minutes. Stir in the flour, scraping the bottom of the pot to incorporate everything. Splash the pan with sherry and add the thyme. Allow the liquid to reduce for 4 to 5 minutes. Add the beef stock, cognac, and salt and pepper to taste and cook for 30 minutes.

Preheat the broiler. Toast the sliced ciabatta, rub each slice with garlic, and place each slice in the bottom of a soup cup or bowl. Add soup to each cup, top with cheese, and place the cups on a rimmed baking sheet or in a large baking pan. Place the pan under the broiler until the cheese melts and the soup is boiling hot, about 1 minute. Serve immediately.

Heirloom Tomato Bisque en Cappuccino

Serves 4 to 6

Don't be surprised if your guests give you a quizzical look when you serve soup in cappuccino cups. Westerners expect large portions (of everything); however, rich soups must be served in small portions. Eat it slowly and enjoy the flavors—there's more food to come!

3 TABLESPOONS BUTTER

1 MEDIUM ONION, MINCED

2 TABLESPOONS ALL-PURPOSE FLOUR

2 CUPS WATER

4 POUNDS HEIRLOOM TOMATOES, PEELED, SEEDED, AND CHOPPED

2 TABLESPOONS LIGHT BROWN SUGAR

6 WHOLE CLOVES

1 TEASPOON SALT

FRESHLY GROUND BLACK PEPPER

1 CUP HEAVY CREAM

Melt the butter in a large saucepan over medium heat. Add the onion and toss to coat. Cook until the onion is tender, about 4 minutes. Sprinkle on the flour and continue cooking and stirring until the mixture foams.

Stir in the water and bring to a boil. Measure out ¾ cup of the chopped tomatoes and set aside. Add the remaining tomato pieces to the boiling mixture, then stir in the brown sugar and cloves.

Reduce the heat to low and cook, uncovered, for 10 minutes. Transfer the mixture to a food mill and force it through. Return it to the saucepan and stir in the reserved tomato pieces. Blend in the salt, pepper, and cream. Warm gently over medium heat, but do not boil. Serve in cappuccino or espresso cups.

PUMPKIN SOUP EN CAPPUCCINO

SERVES 5 TO 6

I have served this soup in cappuccino cups at many dinners. I recommend serving it warm; however, you can serve it chilled in espresso cups as an aperitif when your guests arrive. I really like to use small pie pumpkins or butternut squash that I find at local farmers' markets.

½ CUP OLIVE OIL

1 MEDIUM WHITE ONION, CHOPPED

4 CUPS CANNED PUMPKIN

2 TABLESPOONS BROWN SUGAR

2 CUPS CHICKEN OR VEGETABLE STOCK

CREAM SHERRY

1 CUP HEAVY CREAM

3 TABLESPOONS CHOPPED FRESH BASIL

SALT AND FRESHLY GROUND BLACK PEPPER
   TO TASTE

FROTHED MILK, SOUR CREAM,
   OR HEAVY CREAM, FOR SERVING

Heat the oil in a medium saucepan over medium-low heat. Add the onion and sauté for 5 minutes. Add the pumpkin and brown sugar and stir continuously for 5 to 6 minutes. Transfer the mixture to a food processor or blender and process until smooth then return the mixture to the saucepan.

Stir in the stock and bring to a boil over medium heat. Drizzle with a touch of sherry. Reduce the heat to low and simmer for 5 minutes. Remove from the heat and stir in the cream and basil. The soup can be stored, covered and refrigerated, for up to 2 days. To serve, season the warm or chilled soup with salt and pepper and top with frothed milk, sour cream, or heavy cream.

TUSCAN RIBOLLITA

SERVES 8

Ribollita is a famous soup from Tuscany. Friday's leftover beans become Saturday's minestrone soup, and on Monday you *reboil* it—hence the name! Add crusty bread, more vegetables, and extra virgin olive oil, and you have Ribollita. The Tuscans are *very* frugal people, and nothing is ever wasted. This soup is especially popular during the cold days of winter.

½ CUP OLIVE OIL

2½ CUPS LARGE-DICED SAVOY CABBAGE

1 CUP DICED ONION

1 CUP DICED CARROT

1 CUP DICED GREEN BEANS

2 LARGE STALKS CELERY WITH LEAVES, DICED

1½ CUPS CHOPPED CANNED TOMATOES

2 CUPS DICED POTATOES

6 CUPS WATER OR VEGETABLE STOCK

2½ CUPS BABY SPINACH LEAVES

1 CUP DRAINED CANNED CANNELLINI BEANS

1 CUP GRATED PARMIGIANO-REGGIANO CHEESE, PLUS ADDITIONAL FOR GARNISH

SALT AND FRESHLY CRACKED BLACK PEPPER

SLICES OF GRILLED CRUSTY BREAD

EXTRA VIRGIN OLIVE OIL, FOR GARNISH

Heat the olive oil in a large soup pot. Add the cabbage, onion, carrot, green beans, and celery. Cover and cook over medium-high heat, stirring occasionally to prevent sticking, until the vegetables are softened, about 30 minutes. Add the tomatoes, potatoes, and water and bring to a boil. Lower the heat until the liquid simmers and cook until the vegetables are thoroughly cooked, 20 to 30 more minutes.

Add the spinach, cannellini beans, and grated cheese and stir. Season with salt and pepper to taste. Remove the soup from the heat, cool, and refrigerate overnight.

The next day, reboil the soup and lay slices of grilled bread on top of the soup; drizzle with extra virgin olive oil, sprinkle with extra Parmesan cheese, and stir. Serve hot.

EGGPLANT CAPONATA BAROCCO
SERVES 6 TO 8

This is an old-style Sicilian recipe. Tomatoes were not brought to Italy until the fifteenth century, so there are many old traditional recipes like this one that never contained tomatoes. This is great as an appetizer or as a side dish for your favorite holiday dinner.

½ CUP OLIVE OIL

1 MEDIUM YELLOW ONION, CUBED

½ CUP DICED CELERY

1 LARGE EGGPLANT, PEELED AND CUBED

½ CUP PINOT GRIGIO

2 TABLESPOONS PINE NUTS

2 TABLESPOONS RAISINS

4 TO 5 GREEN OLIVES, PITTED AND QUARTERED

SALT AND FRESHLY GROUND BLACK PEPPER

1 POUND WISCONSIN ASIAGO CHEESE, CUT INTO SMALL CUBES

3 TABLESPOONS CHOPPED FRESH MINT

COCOA POWDER, FOR DUSTING

UNSPRAYED LEMON LEAVES, FOR GARNISH

Heat the olive oil in a large skillet over medium heat. Add the onion, celery, and eggplant and sauté until the eggplant is soft and the onion translucent, about 8 minutes. Add more olive oil if necessary to prevent sticking.

Add the wine and cook to reduce the mixture for about 2 minutes. Add the pine nuts and raisins and continue sautéing for 5 to 8 minutes. Add the olives and salt and pepper to taste. Transfer the mixture to a large mixing bowl and set aside to cool.

Once the mixture has cooled, toss it with the cubed Asiago cheese and chopped mint and dust with the cocoa. Place the chilled lemon leaves in large serving bowls, pour the eggplant mixture on top, and serve.

WISCONSIN BREAD CHEESE PANZANELLA

SERVES 6 TO 8

The traditional cuisine of Tuscany is *la cucina povera* (peasant cooking). The dishes are prepared to minimize waste and maximize the use of leftovers. A true Tuscan chef would *never* throw away bread and would use only seasonal, local ingredients. This recipe is very easy to prepare and is a great way to enjoy a Tuscan tradition. I like to use a variety of local heirloom tomatoes for flavor and color, and adding Wisconsin bread cheese from Carr Valley Cheese puts a twist on a classic recipe.

4 MEDIUM HEIRLOOM TOMATOES

1 MEDIUM CUCUMBER, PEELED

6 TO 8 THICK SLICES CRUSTY ITALIAN BREAD

1 POUND WISCONSIN BREAD CHEESE

1 CUP EXTRA VIRGIN OLIVE OIL

¼ CUP BALSAMIC VINEGAR

2 CLOVES GARLIC, MINCED

SICILIAN SEA SALT AND FRESHLY CRACKED
   BLACK PEPPER

1 MEDIUM RED ONION, SLICED ¼ INCH THICK

½ CUP KALAMATA OLIVES

15 FRESH BASIL LEAVES

Cube the heirloom tomatoes and cucumber and tear the bread into bite-size pieces and set aside. Warm the cheese in the microwave until soft, about 45 seconds, then cut it into large cubes and set aside.

Mix the olive oil, vinegar, and garlic in a large wooden salad bowl. Season with the salt and pepper. Add the torn bread, tomatoes, cucumber, onion slices, olives, and basil leaves. Toss the mixture, adding more olive oil if necessary to moisten it. Top with the cubed cheese and serve.

What exactly is "bread cheese"? It is not made from bread or even meant to be served with bread. Think of it as a toast replacement. It starts out similar to rope cheese and is pressed into a block the size of a slice of bread. The cheese is then toasted until golden brown—it does not melt—and cooled.

SICILIAN GREEN BEAN SALAD

SERVES 6

This salad is, oh, so simple, but yet so traditionally Italian! In the summer, toss it with chopped tomato and olives and serve over warm Italian toast.

2 MEDIUM RED POTATOES, CUT INTO 1-INCH CUBES

1 POUND GREEN BEANS, TRIMMED AND CUT INTO BITE-SIZE PIECES

½ MEDIUM RED ONION, SLICED

½ CUP EXTRA VIRGIN OLIVE OIL

3 TABLESPOONS RED WINE VINEGAR

10 TO 12 FRESH BASIL LEAVES, SLIVERED

SALT AND FRESHLY GROUND BLACK PEPPER

Boil the potatoes in a large stockpot of water until fork-tender, 10 to 20 minutes. Add the green beans and boil for 5 minutes longer. Drain and set aside to cool. Once cooled, add the onion. In a small bowl, whisk together the olive oil, vinegar, and basil. Toss the dressing with the salad and season with salt and pepper to taste before serving.

SPINACH AND GORGONZOLA SALAD

SERVES 4

This salad is a classic that is still on our menu. Depending on the season, we may add fresh berries, oranges, or pineapple. Fresh, crispy croutons always give a nice crunch with the apples.

½ CUP EXTRA VIRGIN OLIVE OIL

1 TABLESPOON HONEY

3 TABLESPOONS BALSAMIC VINEGAR

PINCH OF DRIED OREGANO

4 OUNCES GORGONZOLA CHEESE, CRUMBLED

1 GRANNY SMITH APPLE, CORED AND THINLY SLICED

2 CUPS SPINACH LEAVES

SALT AND FRESHLY CRACKED BLACK PEPPER

Mix the olive oil, honey, vinegar, and oregano in a large bowl. Add the Gorgonzola and sliced apple and stir to coat. Toss with the spinach leaves and serve chilled, seasoned with the salt and pepper.

Jasper's Classic Caesar Salad

Serves 2

This is Jasper's traditional recipe. This is our most popular salad, our most requested recipe, and my family's all-time favorite. I know it will become your favorite too. My father always insisted on serving this salad on a chilled plate with ice-cold forks. If you make this a lot, you'll probably want to invest in a wooden salad bowl with tripod and accessories. They are perfect for making and serving the salad at the table.

Salt

1 clove garlic

3 anchovy fillets

Juice of ½ lemon

2 tablespoons vinegar

½ cup extra virgin olive oil

½ teaspoon Worcestershire sauce

1 egg, beaten

2 cups torn romaine lettuce

1 tablespoon grated Parmigiano-Reggiano cheese

1 cup croutons

Freshly cracked black pepper

Place a little salt in the bottom of a large wooden bowl. Add the peeled garlic and mash well with a fork. Add the anchovies and mash into a paste with the garlic. Mix in the lemon juice. Add the vinegar, oil, and Worcestershire sauce and stir to combine.

In a separate bowl, toss the egg with the lettuce. Transfer the lettuce to the wooden bowl and toss with the dressing. Mix in the cheese and croutons.

Serve the salad on chilled plates with ice-cold forks. Sprinkle freshly cracked pepper on top of each plate of salad.

Note: Thoroughly cooking animal foods such as beef, eggs, fish, lamb, pork, poultry, or shellfish reduces the risk of food-borne illness. Individuals with certain health conditions may be at higher risk if these foods are consumed raw or undercooked. Consult your physician or public health official for further information.

SICILIAN ORANGE AND OLIVE SALAD

SERVES 4

When available, I always use blood oranges in this salad. The preferred blood orange is the Tarocco because of its sweetness and juiciness. It is the most popular table orange in Italy.

1 ½ TEASPOONS OLIVE OIL

2 TABLESPOONS BALSAMIC VINEGAR

PINCH OF SALT

8 TO 10 FRESH BASIL LEAVES

1 CUP JUMBO GREEN OR BLACK OLIVES
(PREFERABLY CRACKED OR CRUSHED)

2 ORANGES, PEELED AND SLICED CROSSWISE

2 TABLESPOONS PINE NUTS

1 RED BELL PEPPER, SEEDED AND CHOPPED

8 LARGE RADICCHIO LETTUCE LEAVES,
FOR SERVING

FRESHLY GROUND BLACK PEPPER

Place the olive oil, vinegar, salt, and basil in a large mixing bowl and mix well. Add the olives and marinate for at least 2 hours or overnight.

Transfer the olive mixture to another mixing bowl and toss with the orange slices, pine nuts, and bell pepper. Place 2 radicchio leaves on each serving plate to act as a cup.

Top each radicchio cup with orange and olive salad and sprinkle with freshly ground pepper.

INSALATA CAPRESE

SERVES 2 TO 3

This is the salad that I served at the James Beard House in New York City. A ripe, good-quality tomato will be firm, smooth skinned, and red. Avoid ones that are too soft, wrinkled, or have split skin. If your Roma tomatoes are not fully ripe, just slice them, dip them in olive oil, and grill them along with the zucchini. This gives a unique flavor to the salad. For an even more unusual option, drizzle some honey on the salad. At the end of the night, leftover salad on crispy Italian bread makes for a great meal!

1 MEDIUM ZUCCHINI, CUT INTO ¼-INCH SLICES

¼ CUP EXTRA VIRGIN OLIVE OIL

1 POUND FRESH MOZZARELLA CHEESE, SLICED ½ INCH THICK

3 RED RIPE TOMATOES, SLICED ½ INCH THICK

¼ CUP BALSAMIC VINEGAR

6 TO 8 FRESH BASIL LEAVES

SALT AND FRESHLY CRACKED BLACK PEPPER

Prepare a charcoal or gas grill or heat a stovetop grill pan.

Dip each slice of zucchini in some of the olive oil and place it on a hot grill over indirect heat or on a hot grill pan over medium-high heat. Cook for 3 to 4 minutes, then turn and cook the other side. Remove from the grill and place on paper towels to absorb the excess oil.

Arrange the zucchini on a platter with the fresh mozzarella and Roma tomato slices. Drizzle with the remaining olive oil and the vinegar and garnish with basil. Add salt and cracked pepper to taste. Serve immediately.

PANZANELLA SALAD

SERVES 4

This is a traditional Tuscan basic recipe that I've been serving for more than 25 years. I learned to make this salad in Florence while attending cooking classes. I like to add heirloom tomatoes and fresh, crisp green beans along with boiled red potatoes. Be creative and use fresh vegetables from the garden and be sure to have fresh oregano or Italian parsley on hand as a nice addition. Remember—you must soak your bread!

1 LARGE LOAF CRUSTY TUSCAN BREAD, CUT INTO 1½-INCH CUBES

1 CUP EXTRA VIRGIN OLIVE OIL

2 POUNDS RIPE TOMATOES, HEIRLOOM PREFERRED, CUT INTO ½-INCH TO ¾-INCH CUBES

½ MEDIUM RED ONION, THINLY SLICED

16 SICILIAN OIL-CURED OLIVES, PITTED

KOSHER SALT

¼ CUP BALSAMIC VINEGAR

10 FRESH BASIL LEAVES

4 SLICES ITALIAN GARLIC TOAST, FOR SERVING

In a large bowl, soak the bread in the olive oil for about 5 minutes. Add the tomatoes, onion, olives, and salt to taste. Mix in the vinegar and basil. Serve the salad over crisp Italian garlic toast.

CALAMARI SALAD

SERVES 6 TO 8

This is a great salad because it can be made several hours in advance. It's a refreshing, fragrant salad with tender squid, fresh basil, and mint to give it a marvelous "summery" feel. Squid is exceedingly tender when cooked properly. Here are a few important things to remember: (1) Be sure to buy the smallest squid available; (2) cook until it loses its rubbery texture; and (3) cook the body of the squid separately from the tentacles to keep the flesh pure white. The skin of the tentacles releases color into the cooking water, which will turn the flesh a pale pink.

COARSE SALT AND FRESHLY GROUND BLACK PEPPER

JUICE OF ½ LEMON

2½ POUNDS SQUID, CLEANED (SEE BOX)

½ CUP FRUITY OLIVE OIL

¼ CUP BALSAMIC VINEGAR

3 CLOVES GARLIC, LIGHTLY CRUSHED

1 TABLESPOON MINCED FRESH BASIL LEAVES

2 TEASPOONS MINCED FRESH MINT LEAVES

Fill 2 separate saucepans with water and add salt and lemon juice to each. Bring to a boil, add the squid bodies to one and the tentacles to the other, and cook both for 20 minutes, or until tender. Drain well and cut the body into rings. Leave the tentacles whole or, if they're large, cut them in half.

Place the squid in a large bowl and toss with the olive oil, vinegar, garlic, and salt and pepper to taste. Cover and marinate in the refrigerator overnight.

Just before serving, sprinkle the squid mixture with the herbs. Toss gently and, if you wish, add salt and pepper to taste. Adjust the dressing, adding more oil and vinegar if necessary.

7 Easy Steps to Clean Squid

1. Carefully pull the head and tentacles from the body sac.
2. Cut the tentacles above the eyes.
3. Pop out the little ball (or beak) in the center of the tentacle and discard it with all the innards.
4. Pull out the quill-shaped bone in the body sac and discard.
5. Peel off the skin.
6. Thoroughly rinse the interior of the body and the tentacles.
7. Drain.

ASPARAGUS SALAD

SERVES 2

Asparagus is low in calories, contains no fat or cholesterol, and is very low in sodium. It is a good source of folic acid, potassium, and dietary fiber. Now let's make it tasty! At Jasper's, we are known for the extra-large asparagus we use in this dish. The sauce is really easy to make and can be used on other vegetables as well.

6 TO 8 THICK ASPARAGUS SPEARS

1 CUP MAYONNAISE

2 TABLESPOONS YELLOW MUSTARD

4 DASHES OF HOT SAUCE

1 TABLESPOON HONEY

¾ CUP HEAVY CREAM

SALT AND FRESHLY GROUND BLACK PEPPER

8 THIN SLICES PROSCIUTTO DI PARMA

Fill a medium bowl with ice water and set it aside. Fill a large pot with water and bring it to a boil. Add the asparagus and cook until crisp-tender. Remove and immediately plunge into the ice water.

In a large mixing bowl, combine the mayonnaise, mustard, hot sauce, honey, cream, and salt and pepper to taste. Mix together thoroughly.

Drain the asparagus and pat it dry. Arrange the asparagus on a plate in a star shape and place a thin slice of prosciutto over each spear, curled nicely. Drizzle a teaspoon of the sauce on each side of the asparagus and serve.

SICILIAN OLIVE SALAD

SERVES 8 TO 10

This traditional Sicilian olive salad has been served at Jasper's for many years and is especially popular in our Italian market, Marco Polo's. Another way to serve this salad is to place the olive mixture in a food processor, pulse 3 to 4 times, and use it as a spread for sandwiches such as a muffaleto or a panini.

3 POUNDS PITTED OR CRACKED GREEN OLIVES

3 SMALL WHITE ONIONS, CHOPPED

¾ TEASPOON SALT

½ TEASPOON FRESHLY GROUND BLACK PEPPER

¼ TEASPOON HOT RED PEPPER FLAKES

3 CLOVES GARLIC, FINELY MINCED

2 TABLESPOONS DRIED OREGANO

1 CUP EXTRA VIRGIN OLIVE OIL

¾ CUP RED WINE VINEGAR

3 STALKS CELERY, CHOPPED

3 CARROTS, SLICED

Place the olives, onions, salt, pepper, hot red pepper flakes, garlic, oregano, olive oil, vinegar, celery, and carrots in a large mixing bowl. Cover and marinate, stirring occasionally, for up to 1 week.

INSALATA ALEXANDRA

SERVES 4

Gorgonzola is a veined Italian blue cheese made from unskimmed cow's milk. It's been around since the early Middle Ages, when it was named for a small town near Milan. I named this salad after my daughter when she was a baby. The first time I made it, she ate it and said it was the best salad she'd ever eaten!

SALAD

- ¾ CUP PECAN PIECES
- 1 POUND MIXED GREENS
- 1 POUND RED GRAPES
- 2 RIPE PEARS, PEELED, CORED, AND CUT INTO THIN BITE-SIZE PIECES
- 8 OUNCES GORGONZOLA CHEESE, CRUMBLED

DRESSING

- 3 CLOVES GARLIC
- ½ CUP HONEY
- ¾ CUP LIGHTLY PACKED FRESH BASIL LEAVES
- ½ TEASPOON FRESHLY GROUND BLACK PEPPER
- ¾ CUP EXTRA VIRGIN OLIVE OIL
- ½ CUP BALSAMIC VINEGAR

Lightly toast the pecan pieces in a dry frying pan over medium heat, tossing for 2 to 3 minutes, making sure the pecan pieces do not burn. Transfer them to a bowl or plate to cool. Place the greens, grapes, pears, and cheese in a salad bowl. Add the cooled pecans and toss to mix.

In a food processor, process the garlic, honey, basil, and pepper until the mixture is finely chopped. Add the oil and vinegar and blend.

Toss the dressing with the greens and serve.

JASPER'S ESCAROLE

SERVES 2

Escarole is a variety of endive, having leaves with irregular frilled edges. I remember the first time I ate escarole. My nana prepared it for my papa, and I thought I had discovered gold, the flavors were so intense. Today my friends join me at our family table and request this with pasta.

3 HEADS FRESH ESCAROLE

¼ CUP EXTRA VIRGIN OLIVE OIL

1 TEASPOON MINCED GARLIC

PINCH OF HOT RED PEPPER FLAKES

PINCH OF SALT

Separate the escarole leaves and boil them in water for 15 minutes, until soft and tender. Remove from the heat, scoop the escarole from the pot, and drain it in a colander. In a sauté pan, heat the oil over medium heat and sauté the garlic for 1 minute. Add the red pepper flakes.

Immediately add the escarole and about ¼ cup of the water from the pot. Sprinkle with salt and sauté for about 4 minutes.

PAPA'S SALAD GREENS AND FIGS

SERVES 4

How I remember my papa's fig tree! He would baby his tree, wrapping it in the fall with straw and black tarp. By late September, the figs tasted like honey, bursting with flavor. Today I eagerly await my first taste of figs each season. It brings back memories of Papa's backyard, staring at his vegetable and fruit gardens, always knowing Nana was cooking something delicious.

½ CUP EXTRA VIRGIN OLIVE OIL

1 CLOVE GARLIC, CRUSHED

¼ CUP BALSAMIC VINEGAR

SALT

2 TABLESPOONS HONEY

8 TO 10 FRESH FIGS, CUT INTO QUARTERS

3 TO 4 CUPS ITALIAN SALAD GREENS

1 CUP MASCARPONE CHEESE

4 TO 8 CROSTINI ROUNDS, FOR SERVING

1 TOMATO, CHOPPED, FOR SERVING

In a medium bowl, whisk together the olive oil, garlic, vinegar, and salt to taste. Slowly add the honey, whisking to combine. Add the figs and let rest by chilling in the refrigerator for 30 minutes.

Divide the salad greens among the individual serving plates and then top with the mascarpone. Lift out the figs from the dressing, scatter them on the salads, and then drizzle the dressing on top of the salads and serve with crostini. Dot each salad with the chopped tomato.

QUIET IN THE KITCHEN!

There is no talking in the kitchen. This was true when my father was in the kitchen, and the tradition continues today. The only person who talks in the kitchen is the person we call "the wheel man." He's the expeditor. He talks to the cooks and places the orders. This way, it's a nice quiet environment so the cooks can focus on the dish that they're preparing.

Whether it's an easy dish, like lasagne, or something a little more complex, like one of our veal dishes with a reduction sauce, it's quiet in the kitchen. There's a saying in the kitchen at Jasper's: "There's only one way to do things, and that's Jasper's way." With my dad, it was either his way or the highway!

The cooks learned over the years that there's only one way to prepare a dish, one recipe to go by, and still, to this day, 55 years later, our treasured recipes are followed exactly. There's no other way to do business. No other chef can come into this kitchen and change a recipe. My brother Leonard is very, very strict about that rule. I've tried to show a little leeway, and he says, "No way!"

That's the way my father was too. He was very detailed. I started off in the kitchen just watching him calling orders, checking each dish as it was prepared. He had a little spoon that he used to check the sauce to make sure that it was just perfect. If it wasn't perfect, he'd tell the chef (in his own way) that it wasn't right, and the chef would start all over again.

CHAPTER 4

PASTA E RISOTTO

What Italian cookbook would be complete without a section on pasta? Leaving that out would be like leaving out a member of your family!

Pasta, like family, comes in many shapes, sizes, and flavors. Take care to treat them gently and don't overcook them. You can, however, throw them up against the wall and see if they have "stick-to-itiveness" if you want.

Here are the basic types and shapes of pasta. (See if you recognize them as anyone in *your* family!):

SHORT: Loves those soups, stews, and casseroles! Small tubular, shell, wheel, and spiral shaped.

MEDIUM: Can't pass up a good thick, chunky sauce or a heavier cream sauce! Tubular with ridges, penne, farfalle (butterflylike), orecchiette, and fusilli (to hold on to those thick, heavier sauces).

WIDE: This one wants more than just sauce. Extra-wide wants multiple ingredients found in lasagne, manicotti, and cannelloni.

LONG: There's one or two in every family—the long, slender ones that will eat only the light, thinner sauces. This includes spaghetti, vermicelli, capellini (angel hair), perciatelli (a spaghetti but hollow and thicker), bucatini (a spaghetti but hollow), tagliatelle, and fettuccine.

FILLED: Say no more! This is the one who eats, enjoys, and hits the recliner chair for a postdinner nap! Some are prefilled, such as tortellini, tortelloni, agnolotti, and ravioli. Others are large, long tubes that you fill yourself, such as cannelloni and manicotti.

Pasta, like family, is the soul of the Italian table, bringing people together for centuries past and centuries to come. It is with pride that I share many of my favorite pasta dishes in this chapter.

THE WALL TEST

For 20 years I always tested the doneness of pasta by throwing it against the wall to see if it would stick. My mother threatened me that she would throw me out of the kitchen if I threw the pasta against the wall. Well, since I was the baby, you know who won! Today things are a little different. I know my wife, Lisa, does not appreciate this technique, but I have convinced my daughter, Alex, that this is the only true test in the Mirabile kitchen. Seriously, though, *al dente* is the way we cook our pasta—"to the tooth." Pasta needs to still have a bit of a bite to it. Overcooked pasta is gummy and tastes mushy (like polenta).

SAUCES

Sauces are the basis of all Italian dishes and a very important part of any recipe. At Jasper's, we try not to oversauce a dish, but some of our customers really like to dip their bread in some of the sauces. As I always say, we are here to please our customers.

Over the years we have made some very traditional sauces and developed a lot of new ones that we have added to our menu. Many of the sauces have been handed down through cousins and family members, and I'm happy to share them with you.

However, there are two sauces that will never appear in any of my cookbooks, and they are Jasper's Shrimp Livornese and Nanni Sauce. We made a promise to my father to keep these recipes family and trade secrets. Only one nonfamily chef has been given the recipe, and he's been with Jasper's for 34 years! Many people call our wives and Mama to try to get the recipes, but they tell them truthfully that even they do not have the recipes.

RISOTTO

Risotto is a rich and creamy, traditional Italian rice dish. It is one of the most common ways of cooking rice in Italy. Its origins are in northern Italy. Properly cooked risotto is rich and creamy but still with some resistance or bite (al dente) and with separate grains. The traditional texture is fairly fluid, or *all'onda* ("wavy"). It should be served on flat dishes, and it should easily spread out, but not have excess watery liquid around the perimeter. It must be eaten at once as it continues to cook in its own heat and can become too dry, with the grains too soft.

My risotto dishes at Jasper's vary depending on the season. Be creative and shop with the seasons, adjusting with seasonal herbs and regional Italian wines. I serve risotto as a first course or as a side dish. On a final note, never walk away from your risotto; always keep an eye on it.

NANA'S BASIC EGG PASTA DOUGH

MAKES 1¼ POUNDS PASTA, SERVES 5 TO 6

This recipe has to be more than 100 years old. It was brought back from the old country by my great-grandmother, who would never consider using store-bought pasta. This pasta is really basic and so easy to make. I like to use it for my ravioli, tortelloni, and pappardelle. Homemade pasta is flavorful, elastic, and very versatile. It's great no matter what sauce you use.

3½ CUPS SIFTED ALL-PURPOSE FLOUR

½ TEASPOON SALT

4 LARGE EGGS

1 TABLESPOON WATER

Place the flour on a wooden board and sprinkle it with the salt. Make a well in the middle and add the eggs and water. Mix with your hands until everything is well combined, adding more flour as needed to make a smooth and elastic but not sticky dough. Divide the dough into 8 balls and let it rest for about 20 minutes.

Follow your pasta machine manufacturer's instructions for rolling and shaping the pasta you wish to make.

Fresh pasta cooks much quicker than dry pasta. I recommend 3 to 4 minutes of cooking time for fresh pasta.

Jasper's Classic Marinara

SERVES 4

This is a good base sauce for many of my recipes. I also like to serve it over pasta, plain and simple. For an added touch, use fresh asparagus, mushrooms, peas, or eggplant. The original recipe calls for anchovies, hence *marinara,* "from the marina"!

¼ CUP OLIVE OIL

¼ MEDIUM ONION, MINCED

4 CLOVES GARLIC, MINCED

PINCH OF SALT

1 (28-OUNCE) CAN CRUSHED SAN MARZANO TOMATOES

6 TO 8 FRESH BASIL LEAVES, TORN

¼ TEASPOON HOT RED PEPPER FLAKES

Heat the olive oil in a shallow pan over medium heat. Add the onion and sauté until translucent, about 5 minutes. Add the garlic and salt and continue to sauté for 1 to 2 minutes. Be sure the garlic does not burn. Add the crushed tomatoes, basil, and red pepper flakes and cook for 25 minutes.

MIRABILE FAMILY SUNDAY SAUCE
SERVES 8

    This is the old-fashioned sauce used by Jasper's and Marco Polo's. If you do not like canned puree, you can substitute whole tomatoes, omit the water, and puree the tomatoes in a food processor or by hand. Make sure you continuously stir the sauce and do not let the sugar burn or you will scorch the sauce. You can also buy this sauce premade at Jasper's.

4 TABLESPOONS EXTRA VIRGIN OLIVE OIL

2 MEDIUM ONIONS, CHOPPED

1 WHOLE HEAD GARLIC CLOVES, PURÉED

1 (28-OUNCE) CAN TOMATO PURÉE

4 CUPS WATER

1 TEASPOON SALT

½ TEASPOON HOT RED PEPPER FLAKES

2 TABLESPOONS FENNEL SEEDS

2 TABLESPOONS SUGAR

10 TO 12 FRESH BASIL LEAVES

Heat the olive oil in a 4-quart pot over medium heat. Add the onions and sauté until translucent, about 15 minutes. Add the garlic and remove the pan from the stove. Add the tomato purée and water and mix thoroughly. Stir in the salt, red pepper flakes, and fennel seeds and cook for about 2 hours, adding the sugar and basil after 1½ hours. At that time you can also add sautéed sausage, meatballs, or braciole.

SUMMER SAUCE

SERVES 4 TO 6

This is our most popular "uncooked" tomato sauce. It's great on pasta, grilled fish, or chops. You may want to add fresh mint for flavor or even some lemon if you marinate chops in the sauce.

1 CUP EXTRA VIRGIN OLIVE OIL

6 CLOVES GARLIC, MINCED

5 POUNDS FRESH TOMATOES, HEIRLOOM
PREFERRED, PEELED AND CRUSHED

20 FRESH BASIL LEAVES, HALVED

½ TEASPOON SALT

½ TEASPOON HOT RED PEPPER FLAKES

Heat the olive oil in a large skillet over medium-high heat. Add the garlic and sauté for 1 minute.

Combine the tomatoes, basil, salt, and red pepper flakes in a large bowl. Mix by hand, crushing the tomatoes as you're mixing. Add the olive oil and garlic, cover the bowl, and let the sauce sit for 2 to 3 hours before serving.

Jasper's Bolognese Sauce

Serves 6

This traditional meat sauce is full of flavor. To add even more flavor, I recommend adding Italian sausage. The carrot is important to the recipe because, when cooked slowly, it becomes sweet and strengthens the sauce. My family likes to serve this over cut pasta such as rigatoni or penne, but I love it tossed with wide egg pappardelle.

2 TABLESPOONS BUTTER

2 TABLESPOONS OLIVE OIL

½ CUP FINELY CHOPPED ONION

1 CELERY STALK, FINELY CHOPPED

½ CUP FINELY CHOPPED CARROT

4 OUNCES PANCETTA, DICED

3 CLOVES GARLIC

1½ POUNDS GROUND BEEF
    OR BULK ITALIAN SAUSAGE

1 TEASPOON SALT

½ TEASPOON HOT RED PEPPER FLAKES

1 CUP CHIANTI

1 (28-OUNCE) CAN SAN MARZANO
    CRUSHED TOMATOES

1 TABLESPOON TOMATO PASTE

10 TO 12 FRESH BASIL LEAVES

PINCH OF FRESHLY GRATED NUTMEG

½ CUP MILK

Melt the butter with the oil in a large saucepan over medium heat. Add the onion, celery, carrot, and pancetta. Cook until the onion is lightly browned, stirring occasionally, about 8 minutes. Stir in the garlic and ground beef and cook until the ground beef is no longer pink. Add the salt and red pepper flakes.

Increase the heat to medium-high, add the Chianti, and simmer until the wine has evaporated, 8 to 10 minutes.

Puree the tomatoes in a food processor. Add them to the meat sauce along with the tomato paste.

Lower the heat to medium-low, cover, and simmer for 45 minutes, or until the sauce thickens. Add the basil and nutmeg and cook for another 15 minutes, stirring occasionally. Stir in the milk and cook for 3 to 4 more minutes. Serve hot.

CLASSIC PESTO

SERVES 10

Have you ever wondered where the name *pesto* came from? It means "pounded." Basic pesto sauce is made with mashed fresh basil leaves, olive oil, pine nuts or walnuts, and Pecorino cheese. You can add other things to expand on it. My pesto sauce is excellent served chilled over various cuts of pasta. It's also good with egg noodle pasta. The true Genovese pesto sauce includes diced potatoes and green beans.

3 CLOVES GARLIC, CHOPPED

½ CUP PINE NUTS

1 TEASPOON SALT

2½ CUPS FRESH BASIL, PURÉED

1 CUP HEAVY CREAM

⅔ CUP EXTRA VIRGIN OLIVE OIL

½ CUP GRATED PARMIGIANO-REGGIANO CHEESE

Put the garlic, pine nuts, and salt in a mortar and use a pestle to pound the mixture to a very fine consistency. Add the basil and continue to pound into a paste.

Place the mixture in a mixing bowl along with the cream, olive oil, and cheese and stir the mixture into a smooth, fine sauce. Transfer the sauce to a sauté pan and warm it over low heat.

Once the sauce is warm, toss it with your favorite pasta until the pasta is well coated. Or serve it cold as a sauce for salads, sandwiches, meats, or seafood.

SICILIAN PESTO ALLA TRAPANI

SERVES 4

I discovered this dish in 2008 while traveling to Sicily with my Slow Food Convivium. It's a classic Sicilian recipe and so simple to prepare! Serve over linguine or spaghetti.

4 CUPS TIGHTLY PACKED FRESH BASIL

1 CUP CHOPPED ITALIAN PARSLEY

4 CLOVES GARLIC, PEELED

1 CUP PINE NUTS, TOASTED

1 CUP ALMONDS, TOASTED

1 CUP GRATED ROMANO CHEESE
(ABOUT 4 OUNCES)

10 CHERRY TOMATOES

½ TEASPOON SALT

1 CUP EXTRA VIRGIN OLIVE OIL

Put all the ingredients in a blender and blend for 1 minute.

Note: To toast almonds and pine nuts, add the nuts to a sauté pan and toss over medium heat until golden, lightly browned, and fragrant, 4 to 5 minutes, taking care not to burn them.

SICILIAN SAUSAGE SUGO

SERVES 6

This is a wonderfully versatile sauce that is perfect over Ricotta Gnocchi (page 88).

1 TABLESPOON BUTTER

½ CUP SLICED SHIITAKE MUSHROOM CAPS

1 POUND ITALIAN SAUSAGE, CRUMBLED

1 CUP SICILIAN NERO D'AVOLA WINE

1 (28-OUNCE) CAN ITALIAN TOMATOES, UNDRAINED

HOT RED PEPPER FLAKES

Melt the butter in a large sauté pan over medium-high heat. Add the mushrooms and sausage and sauté until the sausage is cooked through. Stir in the wine and cook to reduce the liquid, about 15 minutes. Add the tomatoes with their liquid and red pepper flakes to taste.

BÉCHAMEL SAUCE

MAKES 3½ CUPS

This is a wonderful basic white sauce but with much more flavor. A little secret: Add ¼ cup cream sherry at the end and blend by hand with a whisk.

3 CUPS MILK

1 TABLESPOON FINELY CHOPPED ONION

⅛ TEASPOON FRESHLY GRATED NUTMEG

½ TEASPOON FRESHLY GROUND BLACK PEPPER

4 TABLESPOONS (½ STICK) UNSALTED BUTTER

¼ CUP PLUS 2 TABLESPOONS ALL-PURPOSE FLOUR

Combine the milk, onion, nutmeg, and pepper in a small saucepan and bring to a boil over moderate heat. Immediately remove the pan from the heat, cover tightly, and set aside for 10 minutes.

Melt the butter in a heavy 2-quart saucepan over low heat. Remove the pan from the heat and stir in the flour with a wire whisk until you've made a smooth roux. Return the pan to low heat, stirring constantly, and cook for 2 minutes, or until the roux foams.

Pour the milk mixture into the roux and beat vigorously with a whisk until thoroughly blended. Scrape the sides of the pan to make sure all the roux is incorporated into the sauce.

Increase the heat to moderate and, still stirring constantly, cook until the béchamel sauce comes to a boil and thickens enough to coat the wires of the whisk heavily. Reduce the heat and simmer the sauce for 3 to 4 minutes. Remove from the heat and strain the sauce through a fine sieve set over a bowl.

PASTA ALLA NORMA

SERVES 4 TO 5

This was one of the first pastas I discovered during my travels to Sicily. I first tasted this style of preparation at La Scudera, a famous restaurant in Palermo, Sicily. You can make this dish ahead of time and warm it just before serving. I sometimes use a béchamel sauce instead of the tomato sauce.

2 LARGE EGGPLANT

SALT

1 CUP OLIVE OIL

1 POUND ANGEL HAIR PASTA, COOKED ACCORDING TO THE PACKAGE DIRECTIONS

4 CUPS MIRABILE FAMILY SUNDAY SAUCE (PAGE 60)

½ CUP FRESH MOZZARELLA CHEESE, DICED

4 TEASPOONS GRATED PARMIGIANO-REGGIANO CHEESE

10 TO 12 FRESH BASIL LEAVES

Preheat the oven to 450°F.

Slice the eggplant ¼ inch thick and lightly salt each slice. Heat the olive oil in a large skillet over medium heat and sauté the eggplant for 6 to 8 minutes on each side, until fork-tender. Transfer the eggplant to paper towels and pat off the excess oil.

In a large sauté pan over medium heat, toss the angel hair pasta with 24 ounces of the Sunday sauce until the mixture is warmed through.

Arrange the eggplant on the bottom of a 9 by 13-inch baking pan and top each slice of eggplant with pasta. Sprinkle with both cheeses and top with more sauce.

Bake for 15 to 20 minutes, or until the cheese is golden and bubbling. Garnish with fresh basil. Serve at once.

Pasta alla Carbonara

Serve 2 to 3

I have a particular fondness for this pasta dish. Every visit to Rome with my father included a stop at La Carbonara Ristorante in the Campo dei Fiori for this famous pasta preparation. This is one of the most frequently requested dishes at Jasper's. It is not on our everyday menu, but those customers in the know always ask me for this classic recipe. My fifth-grade teacher, Mrs. Gacom, always praised my father's restaurant when she lived in Kansas City, and this was her favorite dish. Whenever she and her family visit Kansas City, they head to Jasper's for this pasta. And whenever I visit Rome, I still head to La Carbonara Ristorante!

SALT

8 OUNCES SPAGHETTI

4 EGG YOLKS

¼ CUP CREAM SHERRY

FRESHLY GROUND BLACK PEPPER

4 TABLESPOONS (½ STICK) BUTTER

½ CUP DICED ONION

1 CUP DICED PANCETTA

¼ CUP GRATED PARMIGIANO-REGGIANO CHEESE

Bring 4 quarts of salted water to a boil in a large pot over high heat. Cook the pasta according to the package directions and drain it in a colander. Do not rinse the pasta as this will cause it to lose its flavor and starch.

While the pasta is cooking, beat the egg yolks with the sherry and a little pepper in a small mixing bowl and set aside.

Melt the butter in a large sauté pan over medium heat. Add the onion and pancetta and sauté for about 4 minutes to render the fat and crisp the pancetta.

Immediately transfer the pasta to the sauté pan with the onion and pancetta. Remove the pan from the heat and stir in the egg yolk mixture. Add the Parmigiano-Reggiano and toss to coat the pasta. Add salt to taste and serve immediately with more freshly ground pepper.

Spaghetti alla Puttanesca

SERVES 4

Puttanesca is a derivation of *puttana*, which means "prostitute." This makes the various stories behind the origin of the name of this dish very interesting. Whatever the truth, puttanesca sauce is great with poached halibut or lemon sole. Sautéed shrimp and scallops make a nice addition to the sauce.

1 CUP OLIVE OIL

6 ANCHOVY FILLETS, DICED

½ CUP BLACK OLIVES, PITTED AND DICED

2 TABLESPOONS DRAINED CAPERS

4 CUPS JASPER'S CLASSIC MARINARA (PAGE 59)

1 POUND SPAGHETTI, COOKED ACCORDING TO THE PACKAGE DIRECTIONS

1 TABLESPOON CHOPPED ITALIAN PARSLEY

¼ TEASPOON HOT RED PEPPER FLAKES

SALT AND FRESHLY GROUND BLACK PEPPER

Heat the olive oil in a large sauté pan over medium-high heat. Add the anchovies and olives and sauté for about 4 minutes. Add the capers and sauce and simmer for 5 minutes. Reduce the heat to low, add the cooked pasta, and mix well. Sprinkle with parsley and red pepper flakes, season with salt and pepper to taste, and serve hot.

SICILIAN PASTA CON SARDE

SERVES 4 TO 6

This is the most popular and well-known Sicilian pasta dish. The toasted bread crumbs are a must, as they represent the wood shavings of St. Joseph, who was a carpenter.

½ CUP RAISINS

1 CUP WARM WATER

1 POUND CAULIFLOWER

1 POUND PASTA, PREFERABLY BUCATINI
   OR THICK MACARONI

½ CUP EXTRA VIRGIN OLIVE OIL

1 MEDIUM ONION, FINELY DICED

1 TEASPOON CHOPPED GARLIC

10 TO 12 DRAINED CANNED SARDINES

1 FENNEL BULB, BOILED AND DICED
   (SEE NOTE)

½ CUP PINE NUTS

2 (28-OUNCE) CANS TOMATO PUREE

10 TO 12 FRESH BASIL LEAVES OR
   1 TEASPOON DRIED, OR MORE TO TASTE

HOT RED PEPPER FLAKES

½ TEASPOON SALT

2 TABLESPOONS GRATED PECORINO
   ROMANO CHEESE

½ CUP TOASTED BREAD CRUMBS

Soak the raisins in the warm water for 30 minutes, then drain and set aside.

Remove the outer green leaves and the core from the stalk end of the cauliflower. Break the cauliflower into pieces and then break off florets. They must be very small to cook quickly.

Bring 4 quarts of salted water to a boil in a large pot over high heat. Add the pasta and cauliflower. Cook for 5 to 8 minutes, or until the cauliflower is tender. Drain and set aside.

Heat the olive oil in a large skillet over medium heat. Add the onion and sauté until translucent, about 5 minutes. Add the garlic and cook for 1 minute. Stir in the sardines, raisins, and fennel.

In a separate pan over high heat, toast the pine nuts for 3 minutes, or until lightly browned. Add them to the onion and garlic and sauté for a few minutes. Stir in the tomato purée and season with the basil, red pepper flakes, and salt. Simmer, stirring occasionally, for 8 to 10 minutes.

Combine the sauce with the pasta and cauliflower and toss to mix. Add more fresh basil if desired. Sprinkle with the cheese and toasted bread crumbs and serve hot.

Note: To boil the fennel bulb, bring 2 quarts of water to a boil over medium heat. Place the cleaned and trimmed fennel bulb in the water and boil until soft, 15 to 20 minutes. Remove the bulb from the water and set it aside to cool. Once it is cool, dice it into bite-size pieces.

BUCATINI ALL'AMATRICIANA

SERVES 4 TO 5

Although this dish is usually credited to the Romans, it was created in the Marches and Umbria, in the town of Amatrice. In Amatrice they also serve it over the fatter bucatini with a hole in the middle. It is traditionally prepared on the first Sunday after the Italian public holiday of August 15.

¼ CUP PLUS 2 TABLESPOONS CHOPPED PROSCIUTTO DI PARMA

6 SLICES BACON, CHOPPED

½ CUP CHOPPED ONION

2 TEASPOONS MINCED GARLIC

PINCH OF HOT RED PEPPER FLAKES

PINCH OF SALT

6 TO 7 CUPS JASPER'S CLASSIC MARINARA (PAGE 59)

1 POUND BUCATINI

¼ CUP GRATED PECORINO ROMANO CHEESE

In a sauté pan over medium-high heat, sauté the prosciutto, bacon, and onion together until the onion is translucent and the bacon crispy, 5 to 6 minutes. Add the garlic and red pepper flakes and cook for 3 minutes. Add the salt and marinara sauce and cook for 4 to 5 minutes.

Meanwhile, cook the pasta according to the package directions. Drain. Spoon the sauce over the pasta and top with the grated Pecorino Romano before serving.

LINGUINE SAN REMO

SERVES 2 TO 3

San Remo is the capital of the Italian Riviera of Flowers and one of my favorite vacation destinations. It's a village of fishermen, and this recipe is a perfect tribute to such a beautiful village. This dish is still on my menu today. I recommend adding calamari and mussels for even more flavor.

¼ CUP OLIVE OIL

6 TO 8 MEDIUM TO LARGE SHRIMP, PEELED

6 TO 8 SEA SCALLOPS

3 OUNCES CLEANED CRAB LEGS, CHOPPED

3 OUNCES LOBSTER MEAT

ALL-PURPOSE FLOUR, FOR DREDGING

1 TEASPOON MINCED GARLIC

1¼ CUPS JASPER'S CLASSIC MARINARA (PAGE 59)

½ CUP HEAVY CREAM

SALT AND FRESHLY GROUND BLACK PEPPER

PINCH OF HOT RED PEPPER FLAKES

8 OUNCES LINGUINE, COOKED ACCORDING TO THE PACKAGE DIRECTIONS

Heat the olive oil in a large sauté pan over medium-high heat. Dredge the seafood in the flour, add it to the pan, and sauté for 3 minutes. Add the garlic and cook for 1 minute. Stir in the marinara sauce and cream and cook for 2 to 3 minutes. Add the salt, pepper, and red pepper flakes to taste and serve over freshly cooked linguine.

LINGUINE AND CLAMS

SERVE 4

My family has been making this classic dish for more than 75 years. Never put cream or cheese in this dish. In Italy it would be a sin! If you cannot find fresh clams, a 16-ounce can of clams can be substituted.

2 POUNDS LITTLENECK CLAMS, SCRUBBED CLEAN

½ CUP OLIVE OIL

4 CLOVES GARLIC, THINLY SLICED

¼ CUP WHITE WINE

1 CUP CLAM JUICE

1 TABLESPOON CHOPPED ITALIAN PARSLEY

PINCH OF HOT RED PEPPER FLAKES

PINCH OF DRIED OREGANO

1 POUND LINGUINE, COOKED ACCORDING TO THE PACKAGE DIRECTIONS

Fill a large pot with ½ inch of water and place it on the stove over high heat. Add the clams and steam them, covered, until they open, usually 3 to 4 minutes. Remove them from the pot, discarding any that do not open, and place them in a large skillet with the olive oil and garlic. Sauté over medium-high heat for 1 to 2 minutes.

Add the wine, clam juice, parsley, red pepper flakes, and oregano and serve over the freshly cooked linguine.

Fettuccine Pope John XXIII

SERVES 2

My father discovered this dish in the early sixties while in Rome. He was dining at a restaurant near the Vatican, and the owner made him a dish that he had created for the pope. When my father came home, he re-created the dish and started serving it to his friends. Our family priest, Fr. Michael Marclewski, S.J., absolutely loves this pasta and even did a radio commercial back in the seventies for my father, telling customers how my father discovered the dish in Rome.

4 OUNCES GREEN FETTUCCINE

4 OUNCES EGG FETTUCCINE

8 TABLESPOONS (1 STICK) BUTTER

1 CUP DICED PROSCIUTTO DI PARMA

2 CUPS HEAVY CREAM

2 CUPS PEAS

1 EGG YOLK

¼ CUP GRATED PARMIGIANO-REGGIANO CHEESE

FRESHLY GROUND BLACK PEPPER

Bring a large pot of water to a boil and cook the pasta until al dente. Drain.

Melt the butter in a large skillet over medium-high heat. Add the prosciutto and sauté for 3 to 5 minutes, until crispy. Stir in the cream and bring the sauce to a boil. Remove the pan from the heat and add the cooked pasta, peas, egg yolk, and cheese. Toss well and sprinkle with pepper before serving.

JASPER'S FETTUCCINE CON PARMIGIANO

SERVES 2 TO 3

You'll hear people say that this dish, a traditional recipe from Alfredo's of Rome, is one of the simplest dishes to make. That's probably true, but at Jasper's we've always done it with showmanship! This dish was very popular in the seventies, and we always prepared it tableside at Jasper's in a silver pan and burner on a table cart. Now, for greater consistency, we prepare it in our kitchen. Today our customers request added ingredients such as broccoli, mushrooms, and grilled chicken.

8 OUNCES FETTUCCINE

4 TABLESPOONS (½ STICK) BUTTER

2 CUPS HEAVY CREAM

1 CUP GRATED PARMIGIANO-REGGIANO CHEESE

SALT AND FRESHLY GROUND BLACK PEPPER

Fill a pot with 2½ to 3 quarts of water, bring it to a boil, and cook the pasta until al dente. Drain and set aside.

Heat the butter and cream over medium-high heat in a pan large enough to hold the pasta. Add the pasta to the pan and heat for 1 to 2 minutes. Add the cheese and heat for 2 more minutes. Toss gently, being careful not to break the pasta. Add salt and pepper to taste and serve hot.

JASPER'S PASTICCIO DI MELANZANE E RICOTTA

SERVES 8 TO 10

This unique lasagne is one that I serve during the winter months. It is also good with cooked spinach layered in between the eggplant.

3 POUNDS RICOTTA CHEESE

5 EGGS

¼ CUP CHOPPED ITALIAN PARSLEY

1 CUP OLIVE OIL

½ TEASPOON SALT

½ TEASPOON FRESHLY GROUND BLACK PEPPER

2 MEDIUM EGGPLANT, SLICED LENGTHWISE ¼ INCH THICK

1½ POUNDS LASAGNE NOODLES

4 TABLESPOONS (½ STICK) BUTTER

6 CUPS BÉCHAMEL SAUCE (PAGE 66)

1 CUP GRATED PARMIGIANO-REGGIANO CHEESE (ABOUT 4 OUNCES)

15 SLICES FRESH MOZZARELLA CHEESE, ¼ INCH THICK

Mix the ricotta, eggs, and parsley together and set aside.

Heat the olive oil in a large skillet over medium heat. Lightly salt and pepper the eggplant and cook for 4 minutes on each side, until golden brown and fork-tender. Transfer the eggplant to paper towels and pat it dry.

Preheat the oven to 350°F.

Cook the lasagne noodles according to the package directions. Drain and set aside.

Coat the bottom of a 10 by 14 by 3-inch baking dish with the butter. Spread a layer of about one-fifth of the béchamel sauce across the bottom, sprinkle with about 3 tablespoons of the Parmesan, and then lay 6 sheets of lasagne noodles on top. Add one-fifth of the ricotta mixture, then a quarter of the mozzarella, followed by a quarter of the eggplant. Repeat this layering process 3 more times.

Spread on a final layer of ricotta and top with the remaining béchamel sauce. Sprinkle with the remaining Parmesan cheese and bake for 45 minutes. Let stand for 10 minutes before cutting. Serve hot.

THE LASAGNE BIRTHDAY CAKE

Every January we celebrate my brother Salvatore's birthday. I've always considered Sam (that's his nickname) the baby of the family, even though I'm the youngest of the brothers. We always say Sam's the baby because he was a mama's boy. That's a good thing in our family, not a bad thing.

When Sam was 7 years old, all the boys were envious because Sam got to have his birthday party at Jasper's. The old Jasper's on 75th wasn't a place where you'd go for dinner every night. It was truly elegant dining, so it was a big deal when Sam got to have his birthday party on a Saturday in the dining room.

Sammy Joe, as he was called when he was younger, always loved lasagne. So Sam had a kids' birthday party in the elegant dining room at Jasper's, along with 12 of his little friends from Christ the King grade school. For his birthday cake, my nana walked through the kitchen to the dining room with a freshly baked pan of lasagne with seven birthday candles on it! Personally, I would have been kind of embarrassed having a birthday cake made out of lasagne, but it was the funniest thing, and Sammy just sat there and smiled. He loved the fact that he got to have his very own lasagne for his birthday.

A few years ago, for his 50th birthday, I surprised Sam with a real birthday cake made to look like a pan of lasagne. I don't know what he thought about it, but anytime we think about lasagne in the Mirabile family we think about that 7th birthday party for Sammy Joe.

Cannelloni Capriccio

Serves 4

This recipe has been on the Jasper's menu for more than 40 years. I have had many customers tell me this is as authentic as any cannelloni they have ever had in Italy. I am so fortunate to have such great customers! Add a touch of tomato sauce to the béchamel and you will have my "pink sauce." Instead of the pasta recipe here, you can use Nana's Basic Egg Pasta Dough (page 58).

Filling

- 4 ounces prosciutto di Parma, finely chopped
- 1 pound ricotta cheese
- 4 ounces bulk Sicilian fennel sausage, cooked
- 2 tablespoons grated Parmigiano-Reggiano cheese
- 2 eggs
- ¼ cup chopped Italian parsley

Pasta

- 2 cups all-purpose flour
- 2 extra-large eggs
- 2 tablespoons olive oil
- Pinch of salt

- 1 egg, beaten with 1 tablespoon water
- 1 cup Béchamel Sauce (page 66)

To make the filling, place the prosciutto, ricotta, cooked sausage, Parmesan, eggs, and parsley in a large mixing bowl and stir until evenly mixed.

To make the pasta, place the flour in a mound on a pastry board. Make a well in the middle and add the eggs, oil, and salt. Mix and knead the dough for 5 to 10 minutes. You can also use a stand mixer with a dough attachment to mix the dough on medium speed for 3 to 4 minutes. Place the dough in a pasta machine and stretch it to ¹⁄₁₆-inch thickness. Cut the sheet of pasta into 6-inch squares.

Preheat the oven to 325°F. To assemble the cannelloni, lay the dough pieces flat on a work surface and dab 2 tablespoons of filling onto each square. Fold two sides of the dough together to form a tube around the filling. Brush the edges with the egg wash and press them together to seal.

Pour ½ cup of the béchamel sauce on the bottom of a baking dish and arrange the cannelloni on top. Top with the remaining ½ cup sauce and bake for 15 to 20 minutes, until golden. Serve piping hot.

Jasper Jr.'s Pumpkin Ravioli

Serves 4 to 6

This is the popular recipe I used on Emeril Lagasse's first TV appearance on the Food Network. In Italy, it is called *ravioli di zucca* and is a favorite in the fall. When I serve this, I like to put a miniature pumpkin on the serving platter for presentation.

RAVIOLI

- 1 CUP PUMPKIN PURÉE
- ¼ CUP GRATED PARMIGIANO-REGGIANO CHEESE
- ½ CUP RICOTTA CHEESE
- PINCH OF FRESHLY GRATED NUTMEG
- 1 EGG
- 2 TABLESPOONS CHOPPED ITALIAN PARSLEY
- 1 POUND NANA'S BASIC EGG PASTA DOUGH (PAGE 58) OR STORE-BOUGHT FRESH PASTA SHEETS

SAUCE

- 1 ½ CUPS HEAVY CREAM
- ½ CUP GRATED PARMIGIANO-REGGIANO CHEESE (ABOUT 2 OUNCES)
- PINCH OF FRESHLY GRATED NUTMEG

- 3 TO 4 HAZELNUTS, CHOPPED, FOR GARNISH

To make the ravioli: In a large bowl, mix the pumpkin purée, Parmesan, ricotta, nutmeg, egg, and parsley. Lay out the pasta sheets and brush the edges with either water or an egg wash made by beating 1 egg with 1 tablespoon of water. Place 1 tablespoon of filling in the middle of each square, fold the square over the filling, and gently press the edges together to seal in the filling. Spray each side of each piece of ravioli with nonstick cooking spray and place it on a sheet of parchment paper. At this point you can put the ravioli in an airtight freezer-safe container and freeze them for up to 1 week before cooking.

To cook the ravioli: Bring at least 3 quarts of water to a boil over high heat. Add the ravioli to the boiling water and cook for 3 to 4 minutes, or until the ravioli float to the top.

While the ravioli are cooking, make the sauce: Mix the cream, cheese, and nutmeg together in a sauté pan and bring to a gentle boil over medium-high heat until the sauce thickens.

Strain the ravioli and add it to the sauce, stirring gently to coat the pasta. Serve on a platter, garnished with hazelnuts.

CRISPY MASCARPONE RIGATONI

SERVES 4

This dish is a tantalizing mixture of flavors and textures! Three types of cheese awaken your taste buds: mascarpone, the fresh sweet cheese typically associated with desserts; Romano, with its sharp, tangy flavor; and, Saxon Creamery Green Fields cheese, an earthy semisoft cheese with sweet nutty tones that vary with the season. The crispy, panfried finish offers your palate a pleasant surprise.

1 POUND RIGATONI

1½ POUNDS CRAVE BROTHERS SWEET
   MASCARPONE

2 TABLESPOONS FINELY CHOPPED FRESH MINT

½ TEASPOON COCOA POWDER

EXTRA VIRGIN OLIVE OIL, FOR DRIZZLING
   AND FRYING

2 CUPS FINE DRY BREAD CRUMBS

2 CUPS JASPER'S CLASSIC MARINARA
   (PAGE 59)

8 TO 10 FRESH BASIL LEAVES, FINELY CHOPPED

8 OUNCES SAXON CREAMERY GREEN FIELDS
   OR PROVOLONE CHEESE, SHAVED

Cook the rigatoni in a large pot of boiling water until al dente. Drain, pat the pasta dry, and set aside.

Whisk the mascarpone with the mint and cocoa in a medium mixing bowl. Spoon the mixture into a pastry bag and fill each rigatoni tube with filling. Drizzle with olive oil and roll in bread crumbs.

Fill a large sauté pan with olive oil about ¼ inch deep and heat to 350°F. Add the rigatoni and fry until crispy on each side, 3 to 4 minutes. Remove and drain on paper towels.

Warm the marinara sauce and place a dollop of it on a serving plate. Arrange 3 to 4 stuffed rigatoni on top of the marinara sauce at various angles. Garnish with chopped basil, sprinkle with shaved cheese, and serve.

Rigatoni alla Caruso

Serves 2 to 3

This is a traditional Neapolitan dish. When I started cooking on the line at Jasper's, this was one of the first dishes that my father let me prepare. I recently put it back on my menu and received a great response from customers.

¼ CUP OLIVE OIL

3 TABLESPOONS SLIVERED ONION

5 TO 6 LARGE MUSHROOMS, SLICED

8 TO 10 LARGE CHICKEN LIVERS

1 CUP Mirabile Family Sunday Sauce (PAGE 60)

2 TABLESPOONS CREAM SHERRY

12 OUNCES RIGATONI, COOKED ACCORDING TO THE PACKAGE DIRECTIONS

Heat the olive oil in a large pan over medium-high heat, add the onion, and sauté until golden, 5 to 6 minutes. Add the mushrooms and cook until tender, about 4 minutes. Add the chicken livers and cook until they're no longer pink. Stir in the tomato sauce and sherry and simmer for about 3 minutes. Serve hot over cooked rigatoni.

PASTA CON MELONE E PROSCIUTTO

SERVES 4

This is one of my own creations and a popular pasta for more than 20 years at Jasper's. It makes you wish summer would last all year! The combination of prosciutto and melon is a natural. I use only cantaloupe. No other melon will work. Do not try to make this dish ahead. It's best served hot.

1 MEDIUM OVERRIPE CANTALOUPE

8 TABLESPOONS (1 STICK) BUTTER

½ CUP DICED PROSCIUTTO DI PARMA

SALT AND FRESHLY GROUND BLACK PEPPER

1½ CUPS HEAVY CREAM

1 POUND RIGATONI, COOKED ACCORDING TO THE PACKAGE DIRECTIONS

1 CUP GRATED PARMIGIANO-REGGIANO CHEESE

Peel and seed the cantaloupe and cut it into ½-inch pieces.

Melt the butter in a large sauté pan over medium-high heat. Add the cantaloupe and prosciutto and sauté until the melon is soft, 3 to 5 minutes. Season with salt and pepper, then add the cream and bring to a boil. Add the pasta and toss until the pasta is coated evenly. Sprinkle in the cheese and mix well. Serve immediately.

PASTA ALLA PRIMAVERA

SERVES 6 TO 8

This is my brother Leonard's recipe and one of my family's favorites. It is great served in *primavera*, or "spring." Be creative with this recipe and use green beans, colored peppers, mushrooms, or other fresh vegetables.

12 TABLESPOONS (1½ STICKS) BUTTER

½ CUP OLIVE OIL

1 CUP CHOPPED CAULIFLOWER

½ MEDIUM ONION, DICED

1 CUP DICED FRESH TOMATO

1 CUP CHOPPED BROCCOLI

1 CUP CUBED ZUCCHINI

½ CUP PEAS

2 TEASPOONS MINCED GARLIC

½ TEASPOON DRIED OREGANO

½ CUP WHITE WINE

SALT AND FRESHLY GROUND BLACK PEPPER

2 CUPS CHICKEN STOCK

1½ POUNDS PENNE OR LINGUINE, COOKED ACCORDING TO THE PACKAGE DIRECTIONS

Melt half the butter with half the olive oil in a large sauté pan. Add the cauliflower and sauté until crisp-tender, about 5 minutes. Add the onion, tomato, broccoli, zucchini, peas, garlic, oregano, and wine. Season with salt and pepper and simmer until the vegetables are al dente, just a few minutes. Add the chicken stock and the remaining olive oil and butter and simmer for about 2 minutes. Sever over penne or linguine.

COUSIN MARIE'S BAKED ZITI

SERVES 4 TO 6

This recipe comes from our cousin Marie Lombardino of New Jersey. I remember visiting Marie and my cousin Carl and their mama and papa, Christine and Paul, when I was very young. They were all such great cooks! My father was treated like a son and brother by the Lombardinos, and we still visit with them often. I use my Sunday Sauce for this dish, but you can use your favorite prepared pasta sauce instead.

1 TABLESPOON OLIVE OIL

1 LARGE YELLOW ONION, DICED

¼ TEASPOON HOT RED PEPPER FLAKES

1 POUND LEAN GROUND BEEF OR BULK ITALIAN SAUSAGE

3 CLOVES GARLIC, MINCED

PINCH OF DRIED OREGANO (OPTIONAL)

3¼ CUPS MIRABILE FAMILY SUNDAY SAUCE (PAGE 60)

1 POUND ZITI, COOKED ACCORDING TO THE PACKAGE DIRECTIONS

½ CUP GRATED PARMIGIANO-REGGIANO CHEESE (ABOUT 2 OUNCES)

1 POUND RICOTTA CHEESE

1 CUP GRATED MOZZARELLA CHEESE (ABOUT 4 OUNCES)

Preheat the oven to 400°F.

Heat the oil in a large pot over medium-low heat. Add the onion and red pepper flakes. Cover and cook until the onion is softened, 5 to 7 minutes.

Add the beef, increase the heat to medium-high, and cook, stirring and breaking it up occasionally, until no trace of pink remains, 5 to 8 minutes. Drain off any remaining liquid. Add the garlic and oregano, if using, and cook for 2 minutes. Add the pasta sauce and heat for 3 minutes.

Remove the pot from the heat, add the cooked pasta, and toss to coat. Add the Parmesan and ricotta and toss again. Spread the mixture in a 9 by 13-inch baking dish and sprinkle with the mozzarella.

Bake until the mozzarella melts, about 15 minutes. Serve hot.

LEONARD'S PASTA AND PORCINI MUSHROOMS

SERVES 4

I served this sauce over sea bass at the James Beard House. At Jasper's we serve this sauce over polenta or tortellini. For even more flavor, add asparagus, fresh mint, and Gorgonzola cheese.

2 CUPS WATER OR CHICKEN BROTH

6 OUNCES DRIED PORCINI MUSHROOMS

8 TABLESPOONS (1 STICK) BUTTER

¼ CUP BRANDY

2 CUPS HEAVY CREAM

¼ TEASPOON HOT RED PEPPER FLAKES

1 TEASPOON SALT

2 TABLESPOONS YELLOW PREPARED MUSTARD

1 TABLESPOON CHOPPED ITALIAN PARSLEY

1 POUND FARFALLE, COOKED TO THE PACKAGE'S DIRECTIONS

1 TABLESPOON PLUS 1 TEASPOON GRATED PARMIGIANO-REGGIANO CHEESE

Bring the water or chicken broth to a boil in a small saucepan. Add the porcini mushrooms, remove the pan from the heat, and steep for 20 to 30 minutes. Drain.

Melt the butter in a medium saucepan over medium-high heat. Add the mushrooms and sauté for 2 to 3 minutes. Add the brandy, cream, red pepper flakes, salt, mustard, and parsley. Continue cooking until the sauce thickens, 4 to 5 minutes.

Add the sauce to the cooked pasta, toss, and sprinkle with the grated Parmesan.

ORECCHIETTE WITH CAULIFLOWER AND CRISPY PANCETTA

SERVES 4

In 1999, Jasper's moved from its original location to a new one. Our theme now is "something old, something new." This is one of our newest dishes, which we run as a special once in a while. It's another old recipe that I have updated and it's one that my customers love. It is so light and flavorful I'm sure you'll love it too.

1 HEAD CAULIFLOWER (1½ POUNDS)

4 OUNCES PANCETTA, DICED

1 CUP OLIVE OIL

3 TO 4 CLOVES GARLIC, PEELED AND FINELY CHOPPED

PINCH OF HOT RED PEPPER FLAKES

PINCH OF DRIED OREGANO

⅓ CUP WATER

8 OUNCES (2 STICKS) BUTTER

1 POUND ORECCHIETTE, COOKED ACCORDING TO THE PACKAGE DIRECTIONS

SALT

Trim the cauliflower and break it into small florets. Bring a large pot of water to a boil, add the cauliflower, and cook over medium-high heat until tender, 10 to 12 minutes. Drain and set aside.

Place the pancetta in a small sauté pan over medium-high heat and sauté until crispy, 3 to 4 minutes. Scoop out the pancetta and drain on paper towels, lightly pressing it with another layer of paper towels to remove excess grease; set aside.

Heat the olive oil in a large sauté pan over medium-high heat. Add the chopped garlic and sauté for 1 minute. Add the cauliflower, red pepper flakes, oregano, water, and butter and cook for 3 to 4 minutes. Add the cooked pasta and the crispy pancetta. Toss to coat, season with salt to taste, and serve warm.

TRUFFLED MACARONI AND CHEESE

SERVES 2 TO 3

Here is a recipe that I make at home for friends and family. I developed this for the Wisconsin Milk Marketing Board for my recipe collection using Wisconsin cheese. This brings mac and cheese to a whole new level.

8 OUNCES MACARONI, COOKED ACCORDING TO THE PACKAGE DIRECTIONS

1 CUP SHREDDED WISCONSIN CHEDDAR CHEESE

3 TABLESPOONS BUTTER, CUT INTO SMALL PIECES, PLUS 1 TABLESPOON FOR THE TOP

¼ CUP CHOPPED SCALLION

1 TEASPOON SALT

⅛ TEASPOON CAYENNE

PINCH OF FRESHLY GRATED NUTMEG

1 CUP SHREDDED FONTINA CHEESE (ABOUT 4 OUNCES)

¼ CUP MILK

¼ CUP HEAVY CREAM

1 EGG

2 TABLESPOONS SWEET SHERRY

½ CUP DRY BREAD CRUMBS

2 TABLESPOONS BLACK OR WHITE TRUFFLE OIL

Preheat the oven to 350°F.

Sprinkle the bottom of a 2-quart baking dish with a layer of one-third each of the cooked macaroni, Cheddar cheese, butter, scallion, salt, cayenne, and nutmeg. Make two more layers, using a third of each of the ingredients for each layer. Scatter the Fontina cheese on top.

In a medium mixing bowl, whisk the milk, cream, egg, and sherry together until smooth. Pour over the top of the pasta, top with the bread crumbs, and dot with the remaining tablespoon of butter. Bake for 25 to 35 minutes, until browned. Drizzle with the truffle oil and serve.

Ricotta Gnocchi

Serves 2 to 3

This is one of my favorite recipes for gnocchi—they come out so light that it's like eating air! Gnocchi ("N'YOH-kee") are dumplings, usually cooked in water but also baked. In Sicily, semolina gnocchi are called *gnocculli*. These gnocchi are great tossed with Sicilian Sausage Sugo (page 65) and topped with a little grated Romano cheese.

1 POUND RICOTTA CHEESE

1 EGG

2 TABLESPOONS GRATED ROMANO CHEESE

2 TABLESPOONS ALL-PURPOSE FLOUR

SEA SALT

In a large mixing bowl, mix the ricotta, egg, Romano, and flour with a spoon. Do not beat or whip. The dough is ready when it no longer sticks to the sides of the bowl. Add more flour if needed. Sprinkle the surface of a pastry board with flour. Using one-quarter of the dough, roll out into a rope about ¾ inch thick. Working quickly, while the dough is still warm, use a knife to cut off ½-inch pieces. Repeat until you have used all the dough. Place the gnocchi on a tray, leaving a space between pieces to prevent them from sticking together.

Bring a large pot of water to a boil, add salt, and drop the gnocchi into the boiling water. Adjust the heat to keep the water at a simmer. The gnocchi are done when they float to the top and are slightly firm to the touch, 3 to 4 minutes. Remove with a slotted spoon. Add your favorite sauce and serve.

Spinach Gnocchi al Forno

Serves 2 to 3

Making gnocchi always requires a bit of guesswork because the moisture content of the dough will vary. Practice makes perfect when it comes to learning how the pasta should look and feel, but it tastes so good you'll want to get a lot of practice! This is also a great way to use leftover spinach.

2 POUNDS FRESH SPINACH

1 POUND RICOTTA CHEESE

3 EGG YOLKS

½ CUP GRATED PARMIGIANO-REGGIANO CHEESE (ABOUT 2 OUNCES), PLUS 1 TABLESPOON

PINCH OF FRESHLY GRATED NUTMEG

SALT AND FRESHLY GROUND BLACK PEPPER

ALL-PURPOSE FLOUR, FOR SHAPING

1½ CUPS BÉCHAMEL SAUCE (PAGE 66)

Wash the spinach thoroughly. In a large pot with a steamer insert, so that the water doesn't directly touch the spinach, steam the spinach over high heat until it is completely wilted, about 5 minutes. Drain the spinach thoroughly and squeeze or press it to remove as much water as possible. Measure out 1 pound of spinach and reserve the remaining spinach for another use.

In a small pan over medium heat, sauté the spinach to dry it as much as possible, but watch it carefully and stir it to make sure it doesn't burn. Once the spinach is as dry as possible, grind it in a food mill using the smallest holed disk while holding the mill directly over a large bowl.

Pass the ricotta through the mill into the spinach and mix well. Add the egg yolks, ½ cup of the Parmesan, the nutmeg, and some salt and pepper. Test the texture with your hands. It's the right texture if you can break off a piece of the mixture and form a small cylindrical shape.

Add flour until you achieve the right texture, usually 2 to 3 tablespoons. The mixture should be moist and sticky. Remember, less flour is better; you don't want to make the mixture too doughy.

Roll one-quarter of the dough into a rope about ¾ inch thick. Working quickly, while the dough is still warm, use a knife to cut off ½-inch pieces. Repeat until you have used all of the dough. Place the gnocchi on a floured tray, leaving a space between pieces to prevent them from sticking together. Let the gnocchi rest while you prepare the water.

Preheat the broiler. Bring 6 quarts of water to a rolling boil in a large pot. Season with salt. The gnocchi are very fragile, so add only a few at a time. Once they rise to the surface, strain them out and place them in an 8 by 10-inch baking dish. Top with the béchamel sauce and the remaining Parmesan. Broil for 2 to 3 minutes, or until the cheese is melted and golden brown.

ASPARAGUS RISOTTO

SERVES 4 TO 6

This risotto cooking technique was introduced by the Arabs, who brought rice to Sicily in the late Middle Ages. Italy's Po Valley proved to be a good place to grow rice, so rice soon became a staple in the Veneto, Lombardia, and Piemonte regions. Every year on April 15, I start going to our local asparagus farm and pick hundreds of pounds of asparagus each week to serve at Jasper's. The taste of local, fresh asparagus is incomparable to that of any other vegetable.

1 POUND ASPARAGUS

3 TABLESPOONS PLUS 1 TEASPOON
   SALTED BUTTER

½ CUP MINCED SHALLOT

1 CUP ARBORIO RICE

½ CUP DRY WHITE WINE

4 TO 5 CUPS CHICKEN STOCK

½ CUP GRATED PARMIGIANO-REGGIANO CHEESE
   (ABOUT 1 POUND)

FRESHLY CRACKED BLACK PEPPER

Break off the tough ends of the asparagus and then cut the spears into 2-inch pieces. Set the tips aside separately.

Melt 3 tablespoons of the butter in a large saucepan over medium-high heat. Add the shallot and sauté until soft, 2 to 3 minutes. Add the asparagus, excluding the tips, and stir in the rice. Cook and stir for 1 minute. Add the wine and bring to a boil, stirring constantly. When all of the wine has been absorbed, add ½ cup of the chicken stock. Reduce the heat to medium and stir constantly until the stock is almost completely absorbed. Continue adding stock ½ cup at a time, cooking and stirring constantly until each ½ cup is absorbed before adding the next, for about 20 minutes, until the rice is al dente.

When ready, the risotto will have a creamy sauce texture. Remove the pan from the heat and add the remaining butter, the Parmesan, asparagus tips, and pepper to taste. Serve at once.

SWEET CORN RISOTTO

SERVES 4

We have such great corn in the Midwest; here is a recipe that shows off our local produce. Italy meets Kansas!

4 TO 5 CUPS CHICKEN STOCK

2 TO 3 EARS CORN, SHUCKED

4 TABLESPOONS (½ STICK) BUTTER

¼ CUP MINCED SCALLION

1 CUP ARBORIO RICE

½ CUP GRATED ROMANO CHEESE (ABOUT 2 OUNCES)

FRESHLY CRACKED BLACK PEPPER TO TASTE

Bring the chicken stock to a boil in a 4-quart pot. Add the corn and cook for 4 to 5 minutes, until just tender. Remove the ears from the stock and set the stock aside. Cut the kernels from the cobs and set the kernels aside.

In another large pot (the one you will use for the risotto), melt 2 tablespoons of the butter. Add the scallion and rice and sauté over medium heat for 2 to 3 minutes. Add the corn kernels. Ladle the hot stock into the rice and corn mixture, one or two ladles at a time, stirring frequently and cooking until each addition is mostly evaporated before adding the next. Add more broth as needed for about 20 minutes, or until the rice is cooked al dente. When the rice is done, add the remaining butter and the cheese. Season with cracked pepper and serve immediately.

TOMATO RISOTTO WITH CRISPY PROSCIUTTO

SERVES 4

Every summer I teach heirloom tomato seminars all around Kansas City, and this is one of the classic recipes that I use. The local heirloom tomatoes at Hen House Market are some of the finest found in America, and I love to support the local farmers.

2 TABLESPOONS OLIVE OIL

1 CUP MINCED ONION

PINCH OF SALT

PINCH OF HOT RED PEPPER FLAKES

6 CUPS WATER OR CHICKEN STOCK

½ TEASPOON CHOPPED GARLIC

4 CUPS ARBORIO RICE

8 OUNCES ASSORTED HEIRLOOM BABY TOMATOES (CHERRY, CURRANT, OR TEARDROP), STEMMED AND CUT IN HALF

1 TABLESPOON BUTTER

¼ CUP HEAVY CREAM (OPTIONAL)

½ CUP GRATED PARMIGIANO-REGGIANO CHEESE (ABOUT 2 OUNCES)

3 TABLESPOONS CHOPPED SCALLION, GREEN PART ONLY

4 OUNCES PROSCIUTTO DI PARMA, DICED AND FRIED UNTIL VERY CRISP

Heat the olive oil in a large sauté pan over medium heat. Add the onion, season with salt and red pepper flakes, and sauté until the onion is slightly soft, about 3 minutes.

Add the water and garlic. Bring the mixture to a boil, reduce the heat to medium, and simmer for about 6 minutes.

Add the rice and simmer for 18 minutes, stirring constantly until the mixture is creamy and bubbly, adding the tomatoes about halfway through the cooking process. Stir in the butter, cream, if using, cheese, and scallion greens and simmer for about 2 minutes, stirring constantly.

Remove the risotto from the heat and spoon it into serving bowls or onto plates. Top each serving with some crispy prosciutto and serve.

FROM NANA'S KITCHEN

We always like to say "From Nana's kitchen" when we refer to our family recipes.

When I was a young child, I would sit at my nana's kitchen table or on the counter, watching her prepare some of her favorite dishes. I'll never forget the times when she made sfinge, these little Italian doughnuts. I'd just sit there and wait while she made the batter and then dropped it in the deep fryer, spoonful by spoonful. When the sfinge rose to the top, she'd put them on paper towels and dust them with confectioners' sugar. Her recipe is on page 143.

My memories of my nana have inspired me to create the same dishes at Jasper's. Some of the recipes we use today are more than 100 years old. My grandmother's grandmother gave some of them to her! Very, very little has changed over the years, and what's great is that it all comes out of the same simple ingredients.

For sfinge, you have flour, oil, water, and a little bit of confectioners' sugar. The end result is a sweet little doughnut that's unbelievably good. Nana always put the sfinge in a little brown sack, and when she'd shake the sack I'd come running. Now, when I have special parties at the restaurant, I give out little brown sacks with warm doughnuts inside, handing a sack to people on the way out so that they get a special little treat and a warm memory of Jasper's. They can have the doughnut for breakfast the next morning—if they can wait!

Many of my ancestors have been in the food business. My grandfather's family had a grocery store. Nana's father had a bakery. Nana herself was from Shreveport, Louisiana, and her cooking always had a southern flair. She made the most wonderful biscuits, chicken cacciatore, old-style tomato sauces, and Sunday ragus, all with that southern touch. She also used what she had: chicken in a red sauce, beef braised in red sauce, fresh lamb—whatever was seasonal, she would cook.

Nana's dishes had a wonderful homey quality. It has nothing to do with the ingredients of the dish. It is a feeling that can be achieved only by a person who has a special connection with cooking, and Nana had a passion for cooking that was surpassed only by her love of sharing it with others. It was a true love affair with her cooking. It was her way of connecting with ancestors long since gone but who came alive through the textures, aromas, and tastes of the dishes she prepared. Fortunately, Nana's passion for cooking was so contagious that she passed it down through the family.

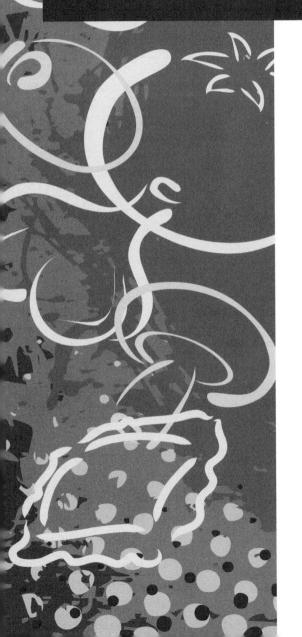

CHAPTER 5

PIATTI DEL GIORNO

T*he main course is another important part of the Italian meal.* We have more than 250 different entrées in the Jasper's recipe collection.

Our menu today has a collection of traditional, timeless classics and new recipes that my father and I compiled before we opened at our new location. Some of the dishes take little time to fix and are simple to prepare, and others take more time and effort. Whatever recipes you try, take your time and enjoy the process of the preparation. Reflect on my family's traditions and realize that some of these recipes are well over a century old and were brought to this country by people with a passion for cooking. Remember this when you are dining at Jasper's too. Take your time and enjoy the ambience, food presentation, aromas, and flavors.

For this chapter, I have selected some of my ancestors' recipes, my personal favorites, and those most popular with our customers to share with you. Whether you are serving them family style for a casual dinner or for special occasions, follow the recipes and I guarantee you will savor the results.

POLLO ALLA FREDERICO
SERVES 8 TO 10

Many of my friends and family know this as "Chicken Fred." My father spent many hours perfecting this recipe, and I am sure he would be proud that I've included it in this book and shared it with you.

½ CUP OLIVE OIL

6 CHICKEN WINGS

5 CHICKEN BREASTS

3 CHICKEN LEGS

4 CHICKEN THIGHS

12 ITALIAN SAUSAGES, HALVED

2 MEDIUM ONIONS, CUT INTO VERY THIN STRIPS

5 RED OR GREEN BELL PEPPERS, SEEDED AND CUT INTO VERY THIN STRIPS

2 CUPS WHITE WINE

1 (28-OUNCE) CAN FINELY DICED TOMATOES (WITH JUICE)

1 (12-OUNCE) CAN PEAS

2 TEASPOONS HOT RED PEPPER FLAKES

1 TEASPOON DRIED BASIL

¾ TEASPOON DRIED TARRAGON

¼ TEASPOON DRIED ROSEMARY

¾ TEASPOON DRIED THYME

5 LARGE POTATOES, PEELED AND CUT INTO 1-INCH CUBES

2 CUPS MUSHROOMS, SLICED

SALT AND FRESHLY GROUND BLACK PEPPER

Preheat the oven to 450°F.

Heat the olive oil in 1 or 2 large sauté pans over high heat. Add the chicken and sausages and sauté for about 10 minutes until brown. Remove the meat and set it aside. In the same pan, sauté the onions and peppers over medium heat until the onions are translucent, 8 to 10 minutes. Place the chicken and sausages in a roasting pan and add the wine, tomatoes (with juice), peas (with juice), red pepper flakes, basil, tarragon, rosemary, and thyme. Stir well.

Bake for 30 minutes. Stir in the potatoes and mushrooms and bake for an additional 30 minutes, until everything is thoroughly cooked. Season with salt and pepper and serve.

POLLO ALLA CHIANTIAGNA

SERVES 4

This is a Tuscan dish that I had many years ago outside Cortona. It is traditionally served with wild rabbit or quail. At Jasper's, I have been using chicken and veal, and my customers really love it. It's great served over your favorite pasta or polenta.

2 TABLESPOONS BUTTER

1 POUND BONELESS, SKINLESS
  CHICKEN BREAST

ALL-PURPOSE FLOUR, FOR DUSTING

¼ CUP OLIVE OIL

2 CLOVES GARLIC, MINCED

16 MUSHROOMS, SLICED

4 OUNCES PROSCIUTTO DI PARMA, DICED

2 CUPS CHIANTI

2 CUPS JASPER'S CLASSIC MARINARA
  (PAGE 59)

Melt the butter in a large skillet over medium-high heat. Cut the chicken into bite-size pieces, dust the pieces with flour, and sauté them for 2 to 3 minutes on each side, until browned and cooked through.

Heat the olive oil in a separate sauté pan over medium-high heat. Add the garlic, mushrooms, and prosciutto and sauté 3 to 4 minutes, or until the mushrooms are soft.

Pour in the Chianti and cook for 5 to 8 minutes to reduce and thicken the sauce. Add the marinara sauce and the cooked chicken, cook for a few minutes to heat everything through, and serve.

POLLO TOSCANINI

SERVES 2

This dish is excellent served over fresh pasta noodles. In winter, I like to serve it with risotto and an array of winter squashes.

4 TABLESPOONS (½ STICK) BUTTER

¼ CUP OLIVE OIL

4 OUNCES BONELESS, SKINLESS CHICKEN BREAST, CUT INTO BITE-SIZE PIECES

4 OUNCES ITALIAN SAUSAGE, CUT INTO BITE-SIZE PIECES

¼ CUP SLICED MUSHROOMS

½ CUP JASPER'S CLASSIC MARINARA (PAGE 59)

¼ CUP BALSAMIC VINEGAR

1 TABLESPOON CHOPPED PITTED BLACK OLIVES

2 TABLESPOONS PEAS

PINCH OF DRIED OREGANO

½ TEASPOON CHOPPED ITALIAN PARSLEY

SALT AND FRESHLY GROUND BLACK PEPPER

Melt the butter with the olive oil in a large saucepan over medium-high heat. Add the chicken and sausage pieces and sauté for 5 to 8 minutes, until lightly browned. Add the mushrooms and cook for another minute. Add the tomato sauce, vinegar, and olives and continue to sauté for 3 to 6 minutes. Add the peas, oregano, and parsley, season to taste with salt and pepper, and lower the heat to simmer the mixture for 5 minutes. Serve immediately.

ROAST CHICKEN WITH 25 CLOVES OF GARLIC

SERVES 3 TO 4

You can save money by cutting up a whole chicken at home rather than buying chicken pieces precut and packaged at the supermarket. The steps to cutting up a whole chicken are quite simple; ask your butcher for a quick lesson or search the Internet for suggestions. The roasted garlic can be squeezed from the skins and spread on bread or eaten. Roasting gives it a really mild flavor that you and your family and guests will enjoy.

25 CLOVES GARLIC, UNPEELED (1 TO 2 HEADS)

1 WHOLE CHICKEN, CUT INTO PIECES

½ CUP WHITE WINE OR APPLE JUICE

½ CUP OLIVE OIL

1 SPRIG ROSEMARY

1 SMALL BUNCH THYME

1 SMALL BUNCH TARRAGON

1 SMALL BUNCH OREGANO

SALT AND FRESHLY GROUND BLACK PEPPER

2 LEMONS

Preheat the oven to 375°F.

Arrange the cloves of garlic across the bottom of a Dutch oven. Place the chicken pieces on top of the garlic, skin side up. Drizzle with the wine and olive oil and arrange all the fresh herbs on top. Sprinkle with salt and pepper. Cut the lemons in half, squeeze the juice over the chicken, and add the lemon halves to the Dutch oven. Cover the Dutch oven tightly.

Bake for 1 hour, or until the juices run clear when a thigh is pricked, removing the lid during the last 10 minutes to brown the chicken if desired.

SICILIAN INVOLTINI

SERVES 4

The first time I ate Sicilian Involtini was in Palermo. As soon as we got home, my father and I perfected this recipe, and it is still on our menu.

2 (8-OUNCE) BONELESS, SKINLESS CHICKEN BREASTS

2 OUNCES PROSCIUTTO HAM, CUT INTO 4 THIN SLICES

2 (4-OUNCE) BALLS FRESH MOZZARELLA CHEESE, THINLY SLICED

1 TEASPOON DRAINED CAPERS

1 TEASPOON RAISINS

2 EGGS, BEATEN

ITALIAN-SEASONED DRY BREAD CRUMBS, FOR DREDGING

¼ CUP OLIVE OIL

SAUCE

¼ CUP WHITE WINE

2 TABLESPOONS BUTTER

JUICE OF ½ LEMON

PINCH OF SALT

¼ CUP FLAVORFUL CHICKEN STOCK

2 SMALL SPRIGS OREGANO

Cut the chicken breasts in half and pound the chicken thin; pat dry. Place a slice of prosciutto on top of each chicken breast, followed by a layer of mozzarella. Sprinkle on the capers and raisins.

Roll the chicken and secure it with a toothpick. Dip the chicken roll in the beaten eggs and then in the bread crumbs.

Heat the olive oil in a large sauté pan over medium-high heat. Add the chicken and cook, turning, until golden brown on all sides, 4 to 5 minutes. Remove the chicken from the pan, discard the toothpick, and arrange the involtini on a hot plate.

To make the sauce, place the wine, butter, lemon juice, salt, chicken stock, and oregano in the same sauté pan you used for the chicken. Heat over medium-high heat until the sauce is well blended and slightly thickened. Drizzle the sauce over the chicken and serve hot.

ROASTED CORNISH HEN WITH BALSAMIC AND DRIED FIG REDUCTION

SERVES 2

This is one of our new dishes at Jasper's, and it is becoming a popular item on the menu. You can substitute dried cherries or cranberries for the figs.

½ CUP BALSAMIC VINEGAR

2 (1½-POUND) CORNISH HENS

½ BLOOD ORANGE, QUARTERED

½ MEDIUM ONION

⅛ TEASPOON SALT

4 TABLESPOONS (½ STICK) BUTTER

¼ CUP PACKED BROWN SUGAR

3 TABLESPOONS WATER

1½ TEASPOONS DRIED ROSEMARY

6 TO 8 SUN-DRIED FIGS, QUARTERED

Preheat the oven to 400°F.

Pour half of the balsamic vinegar into the bottom of a roasting pan. Rinse the Cornish hen and fill the body cavity with the orange and onion. Rub the outside of the hen with the salt and butter. Mix the brown sugar with the water to make a glaze. Pour the glaze over the hen and sprinkle with rosemary. Gently pour the remaining balsamic vinegar over the hen. Arrange the dried figs around the hen. Roast the hen for about 45 minutes, or until golden.

Remove the pan from the oven and transfer the whole hen to a serving platter. Arrange the roasted figs around it and drizzle the hen with the glaze from the bottom of the pan.

JASPER'S MEATBALLS
SERVES 16 TO 18

My favorite saying: "What do I know? I just make meatballs for a living." Oh, but what delicious meatballs they are! In many southern Italian households, Sunday is meatball day. When I was a child, my brothers and I would steal the meatballs as fast as my mother and grandmother could fry them. I continue that cherished tradition today, frying meatballs every Sunday morning for my wife and daughter. As I prepare and fry them, the aroma takes me back to the days of my childhood, and I know that Nana lives on in every dish I create.

2 POUNDS 80 PERCENT LEAN GROUND BEEF

2 LARGE EGGS

1 CUP GRATED PECORINO ROMANO CHEESE (ABOUT 4 OUNCES)

1½ TABLESPOONS CHOPPED ITALIAN PARSLEY

3 CLOVES GARLIC, MINCED

½ CUP MINCED ONION

¼ TEASPOON SALT

¼ TEASPOON FRESHLY GROUND BLACK PEPPER

2 CUPS BREAD CRUMBS

1½ CUPS WATER

1 CUP OLIVE OIL

In a large mixing bowl, combine the beef, eggs, cheese, parsley, garlic, onion, salt, and pepper and mix well. Blend the bread crumbs into the meat mixture. Slowly add all of the water until the mixture is moist.

Shape the meat mixture into 2½ to 3-inch balls.

Heat the oil in a large skillet over medium-high heat. Fry the meatballs in batches, being careful not to crowd the pan. When the bottoms of the meatballs are well browned and slightly crisp, after 5 to 6 minutes, turn and cook the other side for 5 minutes to brown and crisp them.

Remove the meatballs from the heat and drain them on paper towels.

The Piatti di Buon Ricordo
Plates on the Wall

"Hey," customers often ask, "why do you have all of those plates hanging on the wall?"

I have been a fan and collector of the Piatti del Buon Ricordo since 1980. To me, it is a way to keep my visits to Italy with me. Like a secret society, if you go into a restaurant and say, "Buon Ricordo," the restaurant owners know you know!

Buon Ricordo means "good memories," and in Italy time spent at the table in the company of friends is what creates these great memories. You can't just buy a Buon Ricordo plate; you must eat the signature dish the restaurant has chosen. The food is always served on a normal plate, and when you leave you are given the Buon Ricordo plate in a box. Each plate has the name of the restaurant, the featured dish, and the city of origin.

If you walk through Jasper's dining room, you'll see 110 different plates in all. I travel to Italy every year, and each year I collect two or three more when I visit the restaurants. I know I'm not just collecting plates; I'm collecting experiences.

I started collecting these memory plates when I was about 12 years old, when I traveled to Italy with my father for the first time. We were at the Charleston restaurant in Palermo. I had to have this special dish. (Even when I was a little boy, I was always researching and finding out what special dish was offered at each restaurant.) It was the famous pasta dish called Othello. It is made of eggplant layered with several types of sauces and pasta. The plate I received at the Charleston is hanging on the wall at Jasper's today, and you'll find our recipe for Eggplant Othello on page 20.

The plates are like my muse. I'll walk through the dining room and see a plate that will inspire me to go straight to the kitchen and prepare the dish. Guests have often asked if I've had a particular dish on one of the plates. If I have a particular fresh fish, a special pasta, or other unique ingredients required for that dish in my kitchen, I'll create that dish for my customers.

For more information, visit the Web site (www.buonricordo.com). If you love the idea as much as I do, become a member—it is free! By showing your card upon arrival at participating restaurants, you can often receive discounts or free gifts as a preferred member. Be sure to ask for the book with all the listings of the restaurants.

JASPER'S SICILIAN RIB-EYE STEAK PEPERONATA

SERVES 4

In my family, my mom and dad always "breaded" their rib-eyes for flavor. This is an old Sicilian way of cooking. I prefer to add fresh herbs such as basil and mint as garnish and to add flavor.

1 ½ CUPS ITALIAN-SEASONED DRY BREAD CRUMBS

1 TEASPOON CHOPPED GARLIC

½ TEASPOON SALT

1 ½ CUPS OLIVE OIL

2 (16- TO 18-OUNCE) RIB-EYE STEAKS

1 GREEN BELL PEPPER, SEEDED AND SLICED ¼ INCH THICK

1 RED BELL PEPPER, SEEDED AND SLICED ¼ INCH THICK

1 MEDIUM WHITE ONION, CUT INTO ¼-INCH SLICES

PINCH OF SUGAR

PINCH OF HOT RED PEPPER FLAKES

Combine the bread crumbs, garlic, and salt. Pour ½ cup of the olive oil into a bowl. Dip each steak into the olive oil, let the excess drip off, and then dip each steak in the bread crumb mixture, coating all sides. Repeat the dipping process so that the steaks are breaded twice.

Wrap the steaks in wax paper and refrigerate for at least 30 minutes before grilling.

Heat ½ cup of the olive oil in a large sauté pan over medium-high heat. Add the peppers and onion and sauté until the onion is caramelized, about 6 minutes. Add a pinch of sugar and a pinch of red pepper flakes. Set aside.

Heat the remaining ½ cup of olive oil in a separate sauté pan over medium-high heat. Add the steaks and sauté on both sides until they reach your desired doneness. Place the steaks on a serving platter and top with the pepper and onion mixture.

FLAMING PEPPERED KANSAS CITY STEAK

SERVES 4

My father flamed this dish tableside at Jasper's for 40 years. My brothers and I all had to learn how to work the dining room preparing this, Caesar Salad, and Fettuccine Alfredo right there at the table in front of the customers.

4 (14-OUNCE) KANSAS CITY SIRLOIN STRIP STEAKS

SALT AND FRESHLY GROUND BLACK PEPPER

1 TO 2 TABLESPOONS BLACK PEPPERCORNS, CRACKED

4 TABLESPOONS (½ STICK) BUTTER

1 TABLESPOON MINCED SHALLOT

SPLASH OF BRANDY

2 TABLESPOONS ORANGE MARMALADE

1 CUP HEAVY CREAM

⅔ CUP WORCESTERSHIRE SAUCE

Prepare a charcoal or gas grill. Generously season the steaks with salt and then press the cracked pepper into them on both sides. Place on the hot grill and cook to your desired doneness.

Melt the butter in a large sauté pan over high heat. Add the shallot and sauté for 1 to 2 minutes. Carefully add the brandy to the pan and flambé it if you desire. Then add the marmalade and cook for another minute. Add the cream and Worcestershire sauce and simmer until the sauce begins to thicken. Add salt and freshly ground pepper to taste.

Pour the sauce over the steaks and serve immediately.

KANSAS CITY STRIP STEAK AND MAÎTRE D' BUTTER

SERVES 2

OK, I live in Kansas City, and yes, I do think we have the best steakhouses in the United States. So here it is, the secret behind a great steakhouse steak. Fire up the grill or sauté in a pan—either way, it is delicious! Serve with a tossed salad topped with Thousand Island dressing, a 1-pound baked potato, and some Creamed Spinach (page 115) and you have a classic steakhouse dinner, right from your own kitchen. Buon appetito!

MAÎTRE D' BUTTER

- ½ POUND (2 STICKS) BUTTER, AT ROOM TEMPERATURE
- 2 CLOVES GARLIC, MINCED
- 2 TABLESPOONS CHOPPED SHALLOT
- 3 TABLESPOONS CHOPPED ITALIAN PARSLEY

STEAKS

- 1½ TEASPOONS BLACK PEPPERCORNS
- 1½ TEASPOONS GREEN PEPPERCORNS
- 1½ TEASPOONS RED PEPPERCORNS
- ½ TEASPOON GARLIC SALT
- 2 (12-OUNCE) KANSAS CITY STRIP STEAKS

Prepare a charcoal or gas grill (or use a grill pan on top of the stove).

To make the maître d' butter, combine the butter, garlic, shallot, and parsley in a medium mixing bowl and mix well. Place the mixture on a sheet of wax paper and form it into a log. Place in the refrigerator to chill.

Coarsely grind all of the peppercorns. Lightly season the steaks with garlic salt, then press the peppercorns into both sides of the steaks.

Using the grill or a grill pan, cook the steaks for about 5 minutes, or until golden brown. Turn and cook for 5 minutes longer, or until the steaks reach your desired doneness. Place 1 tablespoon of the maître d' butter on each steak just before serving. Leftover maître d' butter can be frozen for up to 3 weeks.

Sunday Braciole with "the Gravy"

Serves 3 to 4

My mama would slowly simmer these stuffed beef rolls in her Sunday gravy. Mama would also put a hard-boiled egg inside the steak before rolling it up. I can still smell the gravy simmering on the stove! When you're making pasta sauce, you can add braciole instead of or along with the meatballs.

1 (2-POUND) BONE-IN BEEF ROUND STEAK

½ CUP OLIVE OIL

3 LARGE CLOVES GARLIC, CHOPPED

2 TABLESPOONS DRIED BASIL

2 TABLESPOONS FRESH ITALIAN PARSLEY

6 TABLESPOONS ROMANO CHEESE, GRATED

6 TABLESPOONS DRIED BREAD CRUMBS

SALT AND FRESHLY GROUND BLACK PEPPER

4 CUPS MIRABILE FAMILY SUNDAY SAUCE (PAGE 60)

Remove the bone from the steak and cut the steak into 6 equal pieces. Place each piece between 2 sheets of wax paper. With a meat mallet, pound each of the steaks to a thickness of about ¼ inch.

Put the olive oil and garlic in a blender and blend at high speed until the garlic is liquefied.

Place the steak pieces on a clean work surface. With a pastry brush, brush all the steak pieces with some of the garlic oil. Spread a teaspoon each of basil and parsley on each piece of steak; add a tablespoon each of cheese and bread crumbs. Season with salt and pepper.

Starting at the narrow end of the steaks, roll each one up jelly-roll style and tie each with kitchen string at both ends and in the middle.

Place the remaining garlic oil in a sauté pan over medium-high heat. Add the steak rolls and cook on all sides until browned, 4 to 5 minutes.

Bring the sauce to a simmer in a 2-quart saucepan over medium-high heat. Add the braciole and allow them to simmer slowly for an hour or more. Remove the strings from the steaks and serve them with "the gravy."

SICILIAN PORK CHOPS

SERVES 4

This is a great recipe for a quick meal. I like to add potatoes, fresh rosemary, and mint and roast the dish slowly.

¼ CUP RAISINS

1 CUP EXTRA VIRGIN OLIVE OIL

2 RED BELL PEPPERS, SEEDED AND SLICED

4 TO 5 HOT CHERRY PEPPERS, SEEDED AND SLICED

¼ CUP PINE NUTS

¼ CUP PINOT GRIGIO

1½ CUPS ITALIAN-SEASONED DRY BREAD CRUMBS

4 TO 6 (5-OUNCE) CENTER-CUT PORK CHOPS

Preheat the oven to 400°F. Soak the raisins in warm water for 5 minutes.

Heat ¼ cup of the olive oil in a large skillet over medium heat. Add the bell peppers, cherry peppers, and pine nuts and sauté for 2 to 3 minutes. Drain the raisins and add to the pepper mixture. Add the wine to the pan and cook to reduce for 3 to 4 minutes. Set aside.

Place the bread crumbs in a large mixing bowl. Dip the pork chops in the remaining olive oil, then press them firmly into the bread crumb mixture to coat each side.

Pour half of the dipping olive oil in the bottom of a large baking dish and then arrange the coated pork chops on top. Drizzle the pork chops with the rest of the dipping olive oil. Bake for 30 minutes, turning the baking dish halfway through the cooking time. Add the pepper mixture and bake for 10 minutes longer.

SLOW-ROASTED PORK LOIN WITH APPLES AND WINE

SERVES 6 TO 8

If you live in the Midwest, you are fortunate to have great cider like the one produced at the Louisburg Cider Mill. Wow, what flavor, and it is unfiltered! The marriage of pork and cider reduced with wine makes for a succulent sauce.

1 (3- TO 4-POUND) BONE-IN PORK LOIN

6 CLOVES GARLIC, CUT INTO SMALL SLIVERS

3 TABLESPOONS EXTRA VIRGIN OLIVE OIL

1 TEASPOON SALT

½ TEASPOON FRESHLY GROUND BLACK PEPPER

LEAVES FROM 4 TO 5 SPRIGS ROSEMARY

½ CUP ORANGE MARMALADE

1 CUP WHITE WINE

1 CUP LOUISBURG APPLE CIDER

4 CRISP GRANNY SMITH APPLES, PEELED, CORED, AND CUT INTO ½-INCH WEDGES

GROUND CINNAMON AND FRESHLY GRATED NUTMEG, FOR DUSTING

Preheat the oven to 350°F.

Rinse the pork loin. Cut several ¼-inch slits in the meat and stuff them with slivers of garlic. Rub the pork loin with the olive oil and season with the salt, pepper, and rosemary. Coat the meat with marmalade, place it in a baking pan, and roast until the internal temperature reaches 150°F on a meat thermometer, about 1¼ hours. Remove from the oven, cover, and let rest for 15 minutes. Reserve the juices from the pan.

Combine the wine and cider in a medium sauté pan. Dust the apple wedges with the cinnamon and nutmeg and add them to the wine and cider. Bring the apple mixture to a boil over medium-high heat, then lower the heat and simmer the mixture, covered, until the apples are tender, about 5 minutes. Add the reserved pork juices and simmer for a few more minutes before removing from the heat.

Slice the pork loin and arrange the slices on individual serving plates. Pour the warm sauce over the pork loin slices and serve.

MARCO POLO'S ITALIAN SAUSAGE, POTATOES, AND PEPPERS

SERVES 2 TO 4

This is the dish that put Marco Polo's on the map! I started grilling sausages on 75th Street in 1984, and this is *the* most requested dish at our market today.

1 MEDIUM WHITE ONION

2 GREEN OR RED BELL PEPPERS

2 MEDIUM IDAHO POTATOES

¼ CUP OLIVE OIL

½ TEASPOON SALT

¼ TEASPOON FRESHLY GROUND BLACK PEPPER

1 POUND SWEET ITALIAN SAUSAGE LINKS

4 HOAGIE ROLLS, CENTERS REMOVED (OPTIONAL)

Prepare a charcoal or gas grill.

Cut the onion crosswise into ½-inch-thick slices. Cut the peppers in half and remove the seeds, then cut them into ½-inch-thick slices. Peel the potatoes and cut them into ¼-inch-thick slices.

Heat the olive oil in a large skillet over medium heat. Add the potatoes and cook for 10 minutes, turning once. Add the peppers and onion and cook for 8 to 10 minutes. Remove from the heat and set aside. Sprinkle with salt and pepper.

On the grill, over low heat, grill the sausages for 20 minutes, or until they are no longer pink in the center. Serve the sausages on a bed of warm onions, peppers, and potatoes or serve the sausages in hoagie rolls, along with some of the onions, peppers, and potatoes.

NANA JO'S GRILLED LAMB CHOPS

SERVES 4 TO 6

Every summer my nana would prepare these delicious little chops on the grill. She would marinate the chops in balsamic vinegar and garlic with a pinch of red pepper flakes. My three brothers and I would eat the chops faster than my dad could take them off the grill!

3 (1-POUND) RACKS OF LAMB

4 TO 5 MINT SPRIGS

½ CUP OLIVE OIL

½ CUP MINT JELLY

2 TO 3 CLOVES GARLIC, THINLY SLICED

PINCH OF RED PEPPER FLAKES

5 TABLESPOONS BALSAMIC VINEGAR

BROWN SUGAR

Trim any excess fat from the racks of lamb and cut away any excess tissue from around the long, thin bones. Cut each rack of lamb along each bone into individual chops. Each 1-pound rack should yield about 8 chops.

In a medium mixing bowl, thoroughly mix the mint, olive oil, mint jelly, garlic, red pepper flakes, vinegar, and brown sugar to taste. Reserve some of the mint sauce in a separate bowl for dipping the cooked chops.

Heat the grill. Place the chops on the grill and cook to your desired doneness, periodically brushing the chops with the mint mixture. Serve the chops hot off the grill with the reserved mint sauce.

OSSO BUCO MILANESE

SERVES 4

The veal shank is called *osso buco* in Italian. Literally, it means "hole bone," because the bone marrow is part of the appeal of the dish. This is a popular dish on our menu. It is slow roasted in our brick oven.

4 TABLESPOONS (½ STICK) BUTTER

4 POUNDS VEAL OSSO BUCO (VEAL SHANKS CUT 3½ INCHES THICK)

¼ CUP BRANDY

2 TEASPOONS SALT

2 MEDIUM ONIONS, CHOPPED

8 TO 10 BABY CARROTS, CHOPPED

2 STALKS CELERY, COARSELY CHOPPED

1 (750 ML) BOTTLE CHIANTI

1 (28-OUNCE) CAN SAN MARZANO TOMATOES, CRUSHED BY HAND

½ TEASPOON HOT RED PEPPER FLAKES

2 SPRIGS ROSEMARY

4 MEDIUM POTATOES, CUT INTO ¾-INCH CUBES

Preheat the oven to 375°F.

Melt the butter in a large skillet over high heat. Sear the veal osso buco on each side, 2 to 3 minutes. Add the brandy and season with the salt.

Toss the onions, carrots, and celery in a large roasting pan. Add the veal shanks, wine, crushed tomatoes, red pepper flakes, and rosemary and stir. Roast for 2 hours and 15 minutes. Add the potatoes and cook for another 45 minutes. Serve at once.

VEAL MILANESE

SERVES 2

Like the ancient Romans, most Italians prefer veal to beef. The people of Milan have a long culinary history. The Cotoletta alla Milanese, or breaded veal cutlet, can be traced back to 1134. This predates the first documentation of Wiener schnitzel. In the 19th century Milan was part of the Austro-Hungarian Empire. A Milanese cook went from Milan to Vienna to work at the court of the emperor. While there, he introduced the veal cutlet to Viennese society, which embraced it with a passion.

1 CUP DRY BREAD CRUMBS

2 CLOVES GARLIC, MINCED

½ CUP GRATED ROMANO CHEESE

2 TABLESPOONS CHOPPED ITALIAN PARSLEY

2 EGGS

8 OUNCES VEAL LEG SLICES, POUNDED THIN

4 TABLESPOONS (½ STICK) UNSALTED BUTTER

2 TABLESPOONS OLIVE OIL

1 LEMON, QUARTERED

In a large mixing bowl, mix the bread crumbs, garlic, cheese, and parsley. In another large mixing bowl, beat the eggs. Dip the veal slices into the beaten eggs and then into the bread crumb mixture, coating them evenly.

Heat the butter and olive oil in a large skillet over medium heat. Add the coated veal and cook for 3 to 4 minutes on each side, until golden brown. Place the veal on plates and garnish with the lemon wedges.

VEAL MARSALA

SERVES 3 TO 4

Marsala wine was discovered by an Englishman visiting Sicily in the 1700s. This Sicilian wine is widely used throughout Italy in everything from appetizers to desserts. I use sweet Marsala for this dish. Marsala is also served in Italy after dinner as a digestive.

1 POUND VEAL LEG SLICES, POUNDED THIN

ALL-PURPOSE FLOUR, FOR DREDGING

2 TABLESPOONS BUTTER

2 TABLESPOONS OLIVE OIL

3 TO 4 OUNCES FRESH PORCINI MUSHROOMS, THINLY SLICED

¼ TO ⅓ CUP MARSALA

SALT

Dredge the veal in the flour. Heat the butter and oil in a large skillet over medium-high heat and sauté the veal for about 2 minutes on each side. Add the mushrooms and Marsala, season with salt, and cook until the sauce thickens, 3 to 4 minutes.

VITELLO FIORENTINA

SERVES 2

This veal dish is prepared in the Florentine style. The creamed spinach is also delicious on its own. You can substitute a boneless pork chop, pounded thin, for the veal.

½ CUP OLIVE OIL

8 OUNCES VEAL LEG SLICES, POUNDED THIN

ALL-PURPOSE FLOUR, FOR DREDGING

⅓ CUP WHITE WINE

JUICE OF 2 LEMONS

2 TABLESPOONS BUTTER

PINCH OF DRIED TARRAGON

SALT AND FRESHLY GROUND BLACK PEPPER

½ CUP CREAMED SPINACH (RECIPE FOLLOWS)

2 TO 3 OUNCES FONTINA CHEESE,
   THINLY SLICED

Heat the olive oil in a large skillet over medium heat. Dredge the veal in the flour and sauté for 2 to 3 minutes on each side.

Add the wine, lemon juice, butter, and tarragon and season with salt and pepper. Top each veal slice with creamed spinach and Fontina cheese. Place the lid on the pan and cook for 3 minutes, or until the cheese melts. Serve the veal on a platter with the sauce drizzled on top.

CREAMED SPINACH

MAKES 3 CUPS

2 POUNDS FRESH SPINACH

3 SLICES PANCETTA, CHOPPED

1 CUP FINELY CHOPPED ONION

1 CLOVE GARLIC, FINELY CHOPPED

1 TABLESPOON ALL-PURPOSE FLOUR

½ TEASPOON SALT

½ TEASPOON FRESHLY GROUND
BLACK PEPPER

1½ CUPS MILK

Bring a large pot of water to a boil, add the spinach, and cook for 4 to 5 minutes, until tender. Drain well and cool.

In a large sauté pan, sauté the pancetta, onion, and garlic together for 10 minutes, or until the onion is tender. Remove the pan from the heat and add the flour, salt, and pepper, mixing well.

Return the pan to the heat and gradually add the milk, stirring until the mixture thickens. Add the spinach and mix well.

VITELLO ALLA VALDOSTANA

SERVES 2 TO 4

The name of this dish is derived from its two most flavorful ingredients—*vitello*, which means "veal," and *Valdostana,* which indicates any variety of dishes from the Valle d'Aosta containing the region's Fontina cheese. You can easily substitute chicken breast for the veal slices.

1 POUND VEAL TENDERLOIN

2 EGGS, BEATEN

4 EXTRA-THIN SLICES PROSCIUTTO DI PARMA

4 SLICES FONTINA CHEESE

20 BABY CAPERS

20 RAISINS

2 TEASPOONS ITALIAN-SEASONED DRY BREAD CRUMBS

½ CUP OLIVE OIL

1 TABLESPOON BUTTER

ALL-PURPOSE FLOUR, FOR DREDGING

¼ CUP CREAM SHERRY

¼ CUP FRESHLY SQUEEZED LEMON JUICE

1 CUP FLAVORFUL VEAL STOCK

SALT AND FRESHLY GROUND BLACK PEPPER TO TASTE

Cut the veal tenderloin into 2-ounce portions. Use a meat mallet to pound 2 of the pieces thin, until they are each about 6 inches long and 4 inches wide. Brush each piece with some of the beaten eggs and place a slice of prosciutto and a slice of cheese on top of one slice. Add 5 of the capers and 5 of the raisins and sprinkle with about ½ teaspoon of the bread crumbs.

Place the other thin slice of veal on top and press down lightly (so it looks like a sandwich). Repeat the process with the remaining veal slices. Place the veal in the refrigerator to allow it to shape and rest for at least 30 minutes. Place the remaining beaten eggs in the refrigerator too.

Remove the veal from the refrigerator. Heat the olive oil and butter in a large skillet over medium-high heat. Dredge one piece of veal lightly in flour and then dip it into the beaten eggs. Place the veal in the skillet and cook for about 2 minutes, or until golden.

Using a spatula, carefully flip it over and sauté the other side for 2 minutes, sprinkling with sherry and lemon juice. Repeat with the remaining veal. You can keep the cooked veal warm by placing it in an oven-safe dish, covering it with aluminum foil, and placing it in a preheated 200°F oven while you cook the remaining pieces of veal and make the pan sauce.

After you remove the last piece of veal from the pan, add the veal stock and some salt and pepper. Cook the sauce for 3 to 4 minutes.

To serve, pour a little bit of the sauce on a serving platter and arrange the veal on top.

VITELLO ALLA LIMONATA DORE

SERVES 2

This is the best Veal Limonata in Kansas City. It is the same recipe that my father shared with Craig Claiborne in his cookbook *Veal Cookery*, and I'm proud to share it with you.

8 VEAL LEG SLICES, ABOUT 1½ POUNDS

SALT AND FRESHLY GROUND BLACK PEPPER

8 OUNCES EGGPLANT, PEELED AND CUT INTO 8 (¼-INCH-THICK) ROUNDS

ALL-PURPOSE FLOUR, FOR DREDGING

2 EGGS, LIGHTLY BEATEN

1 CUP FINE FRESH BREAD CRUMBS

½ CUP PLUS 3 TABLESPOONS OLIVE OIL

8 OUNCES (2 STICKS) BUTTER

¼ CUP CREAM SHERRY

3 TABLESPOONS FRESHLY SQUEEZED LEMON JUICE

8 THIN LEMON SLICES, SEEDED

1 TABLESPOON CHOPPED ITALIAN PARSLEY

PINCH OF DRIED OREGANO

With the flat side of the meat mallet, lightly pound the meat until it is ¼ inch thick, then season it with salt and pepper.

Sprinkle the eggplant rounds with salt and pepper. Dredge them in flour and shake off the excess. Dip the floured eggplant rounds in the eggs and then in the bread crumbs, patting them to help the bread crumbs adhere to the eggplant.

Heat ½ cup of the olive oil in a large skillet over medium-high heat and cook the eggplant slices on both sides until golden brown, 4 to 5 minutes. Drain on paper towels.

Dip the veal in the eggs and coat each piece well. Dip the pieces of veal in the bread crumbs and shake off the excess. Heat the remaining 3 tablespoons of olive oil and the butter in another large skillet over medium-high heat;

cook the veal 2 to 3 pieces at a time until golden brown, about 3 minutes. Turn and cook on the other side, another 3 minutes. Repeat with any remaining pieces of veal until all of the meat is cooked. You can keep the cooked veal warm by placing it in an oven-safe dish, covering it with aluminum foil, and placing it in a preheated 200°F oven while you cook the remaining pieces of veal.

Splash the veal with the sherry and lemon juice and then arrange it on a platter with the slices slightly overlapping. Top each slice with an eggplant round and a lemon slice. Sprinkle with parsley and oregano and serve.

SICILIAN GARLIC CRABS

SERVES 2 TO 3

I had the good fortune to travel to Alaska in 2007 and appear on the Discovery Channel show *Deadliest Catch*, where I met the crews from the *Cornelia Marie* and the *Time Bandit*.

My friend Jon Wissman, from Hen House Market, and I actually broadcast our radio show, *LIVE! From Jasper's Kitchen*, from the deck of the *Cornelia Marie*. It was during that trip that I learned to appreciate *real* Alaska king crab, as well as Alaska king crab fishermen. The Alaska king crab is already highly coveted for its sweet flavor and supple texture. By adding just a few ingredients to enhance the taste, you can create a simple dish that is delectable and satisfying. I like to serve it with warm rolls to soak up the garlic butter.

1½ POUNDS ALASKA KING CRAB

8 TABLESPOONS (1 STICK) BUTTER

3 TABLESPOONS MINCED GARLIC

½ CUP OLIVE OIL

1 TABLESPOON OLD BAY SEASONING

½ CUP FINELY CHOPPED ITALIAN PARSLEY

1 LEMON, HALVED

Crack the crab into 4 pieces and then into 2 sections down the middle. Melt the butter in a large skillet over medium heat. Add the garlic, olive oil, and Old Bay seasoning. Place the crab in the pan, cover, and cook for 4 to 5 minutes.

Remove the crab from the pan, place it on a platter, and top with plenty of chopped parsley. Pour the garlic butter from the skillet onto the crabs and serve with the lemon halves.

PAPA MIRABILE'S SCAMPI

SERVES 3 TO 4

This was my father's traditional shrimp dish. His mother made it on Christmas Eve for the Feast of the Seven Fishes. The caramelized onion and sherry make this dish a wonderful holiday tradition.

8 TABLESPOONS (1 STICK) BUTTER

1 MEDIUM ONION, CUT INTO ¼-INCH SLICES

2 TEASPOONS MINCED GARLIC

1 POUND MEDIUM-SIZE SHRIMP, PEELED AND DEVEINED

½ TEASPOON HOT RED PEPPER FLAKES

3 TABLESPOONS CHOPPED FRESH BASIL

2 TABLESPOONS CHOPPED ITALIAN PARSLEY

¼ TEASPOON SALT

½ CUP CREAM SHERRY

Melt the butter in a large sauté pan over medium-high heat, add the onion, and sauté until caramelized, 6 to 8 minutes. Add the garlic and cook, stirring often so it does not burn, for 1 to 2 minutes. Add the shrimp, red pepper flakes, basil, and parsley and season with salt.

Add the sherry and sauté for 2 to 3 minutes longer, or until the shrimp is tender. Serve at once.

SCAMPI FRA DIAVOLO

SERVES 4

This is a spicy dish. *Fra diavolo* means "from the devil," hot and fiery. Add extra red pepper flakes if you dare! I serve this over pasta or on a platter with crispy bread. My family *really* likes this spicy dish served with a big glass of Amarone wine.

⅓ CUP OLIVE OIL

16 JUMBO SHRIMP, PEELED AND DEVEINED

ALL-PURPOSE FLOUR, FOR DUSTING

½ CUP SLICED FRESH MUSHROOMS

½ TEASPOON CRUSHED GARLIC

¼ CUP WHITE WINE

3 CUPS JASPER'S CLASSIC MARINARA (PAGE 59)

PINCH OF HOT RED PEPPER FLAKES

1 POUND LINGUINI OR SPAGHETTI, COOKED AL DENTE

Heat the olive oil in a large sauté pan over medium-high heat. Lightly dust the shrimp with the flour, add to the pan, and sauté for 2 to 3 minutes on each side.

Add the mushrooms and sauté for another minute. Add the garlic and cook for a minute, then add the wine. Stir in the marinara sauce and the red pepper flakes and cook for 3 to 4 minutes.

Serve the sauce very hot over freshly cooked pasta.

Swordfish and Sicilian Blood Orange Crudo

Serves 2

Crudo is a raw fish dish with olive oil, citrus juices, sea salt, and sometimes vinegar.

Frisée (which means "curly" in French) is a curly lettuce with long leaves that meet at a short whitish stem that looks a lot like the base of the fennel plant. The leaves should be tender and green with no yellowing.

3 BLOOD ORANGES, PREFERABLY SICILIAN

2 (6-OUNCE) SWORDFISH STEAKS, SLICED PAPER-THIN

½ CUP EXTRA VIRGIN OLIVE OIL

1 CUP LIGHTLY PACKED FRISÉE

SICILIAN SEA SALT

½ CUP SHELLED WHOLE PISTACHIOS

2 CROSTINI, FOR SERVING

Peel and section 2 of the blood oranges with a sharp knife, discarding the pith and membrane. Squeeze the juice from the remaining blood orange into a small mixing bowl.

Place the slices of swordfish on a plate and coat them with one-quarter of the blood orange juice, reserving the rest. Place the swordfish in the refrigerator for 2 to 3 hours to marinate.

In a small mixing bowl, whisk the remaining blood orange juice with the olive oil to create a vinaigrette. Set aside.

Arrange the marinated swordfish and the blood orange sections on a chilled serving platter. In a medium mixing bowl, drizzle the frisée with half of the vinaigrette. Sprinkle the swordfish and blood oranges with sea salt, then sprinkle the pistachios on top. Place the frisée in the middle of the platter and drizzle the remaining blood orange vinaigrette on top of the swordfish and blood oranges. Serve with crostini.

THE LAST SUPPER MURAL

When you enter Jasper's and walk through the main dining room, to your left you'll see a mural that spreads across the whole wall. It's called The Last Supper. The artist, Stephen Murillo, was influenced by my father.

We sold the Jasper's location on 75th Street in 1997. Before that time my father wanted to have a grand dinner—a Last Supper, so to speak—for all his good customers over the years. We decided that we would have a big dinner and I would prepare some famous dishes from 40 years' worth of menus at Jasper's. The restaurant was 40 years old at that time. My father didn't want anyone to know we were closing Jasper's (he hated to use the word closing), and it was very hard for my father to close the restaurant where everything had been born. The family came together there, all his recipes started there, the whole thing started there. What began as a five-seat bar and twelve tables grew into a grand restaurant that was known nationwide.

My father knew that my brother Leonard and I wanted to open a new restaurant, so he decided to close the old Jasper's very quietly on June 27 and not tell anybody. The last dinner that was served there was the night my brother James and his wife celebrated their ninth wedding anniversary. I served that dinner at about 11 o'clock, and I'll never forget the lobster livornese, the lobster ravioli, and the peppered steaks. We didn't end up having a last supper for our guests, and I think that really bothered my father.

Over the 18 months that we were closed, we got to know an architect and designer named Matthew Connelly, who connected us with artist Stephen Murillo. Stephen would come over to the house and show my dad different ideas and drawings and sketches of what he wanted. Like many great artists, his mind was all over the room. Though he didn't get a chance to experience the old Jasper's location, he did get a feel for my father's home and how my father lived. My father was not a particularly religious man, but he did have the biblical Last Supper over his dining room table. He had a picture of Jesus in the hallway and another Last Supper on his coffee table. That definitely gave Stephen a hint about what he was going to paint for my dad.

Without even hearing the story about my father's dream to have a grand supper with all his friends and customers, Stephen came up with the mural that you see on the wall today. In the middle, a chef prepares for a grand supper. He's making a pappardelle dish, which was my father's (and is my own) favorite pasta.

Stephen actually painted the mural in his studio and then came to Jasper's and put it on the wall. When he installed the painting, he wasn't aware that my father had passed away. Coincidentally, my father had several representations of The Last Supper *all throughout the coffin in which he was buried.*

We had many big dinners at the old Jasper's. Everyone assisted my father, and he was a great delegator of authority. You wanted to work for him. My father had lots of followers—people who wanted to find out about his ideas on cooking and learn about his ancestors. They were very open to his influence, and my father created memories for them, even if he was just teaching one or two recipes or sharing a story. Many of our former employees have opened up restaurants throughout the country, and they always come back and talk about my father. When we share the story about that mural, it brings back great memories.

The idea of the mural fits with our theme at our current Jasper's location: "Something old; something new." We took traditional, authentic recipes and began a tradition of new recipes from the same family. When I look at the mural on our wall, of course I think of The Last Supper *with Jesus and his twelve disciples, but more than that, I think of my father in the kitchen, cooking for a grand dinner.*

CHAPTER 6

DOLCI

La dolce vita! Italians love their sweets! Dolce are my favorite course. How can you not finish a meal without a sweet?

One of my first jobs at Jasper's was pushing the dessert cart to the tables. For a twelve-year-old, this was exciting because I knew every dessert by heart. I always added that "my mother baked this" or "this is Nana's recipe." My personal favorite is a given—cannoli. Just read the story On the Cannoli Trail (page 150).

At Jasper's all meals are ended with the presentation of our dessert cart, consisting of ricotta cheesecake, tiramisu, tartufo—well, the list goes on and on.

Here are some old-style and new dessert recipes from my collection.

JASPER'S TARTUFO

SERVES 8

This dessert was created in Rome at the world-famous Ristorante Tre Scalini, located in the Piazza Navona, a short walk from the Campo dei Fiori. I ate there many times with my parents, and even today I hit this place every time I go to Rome. You can have your tartufo and stroll around the fountains in what many regard as Rome's most evocative piazza. Or you can sit at one of the tables outside Tre Scalini and do what everybody else is doing—people watch!

1 CUP VANILLA ICE CREAM, SLIGHTLY SOFTENED

8 MARASCHINO CHERRIES

2 CUPS CHOCOLATE ICE CREAM, SLIGHTLY SOFTENED

1 ½ CUPS CHOCOLATE SHAVINGS

CHOCOLATE SYRUP, FOR SERVING

FRESHLY WHIPPED CREAM, FOR SERVING

With a small ice cream scoop, make 8 walnut-size balls of the vanilla ice cream. Place a cherry in the center of each ball, then place the balls in the freezer to harden while you prepare the chocolate ice cream.

With a large ice cream scoop, shave out 8 flat portions of chocolate ice cream, enough to cover the frozen vanilla ice cream balls. Remove the frozen vanilla ice cream mixture and pack the chocolate ice cream around it, completely covering the vanilla ice cream. Freeze for 30 minutes.

Put the chocolate shavings on a piece of wax paper. Remove the frozen tartufo balls from the freezer and roll them in the chocolate shavings. Serve with chocolate syrup and freshly whipped cream.

CANNOLI TARTUFO

SERVES 12

Cannoli are classic Italian pastries that consist of a fried tube-shaped shell filled with ricotta cheese, citron, nuts, and flavorings. We have taken this famous dessert and made an ice cream. You get the same flavors as in the traditional dessert, but in an ice cream that can be served very elegantly in a restaurant or at home.

1 GALLON VANILLA ICE CREAM

2 POUNDS RICOTTA CHEESE

2 CUPS HEAVY CREAM

4 OUNCES DARK CHOCOLATE, CHOPPED

40 WHOLE SHELLED PISTACHIO NUTS

½ CUP FINELY CHOPPED CITRON
   (CANDIED FRUIT)

4 DROPS CINNAMON OIL

2 DROPS CLOVE OIL

1 TEASPOON VANILLA EXTRACT

24 MARASCHINO CHERRIES

FINELY CHOPPED DARK CHOCOLATE,
   FOR ROLLING

WHIPPED CREAM, FOR SERVING

FRESH BERRIES, FOR SERVING

¼ CUP SALSA AL VIN COTTO (PAGE 146)

In a large bowl, soften the vanilla ice cream, but do not let it melt completely.

In a mixer, whip the drained ricotta cheese for 3 minutes, until creamy, and set it aside. Pour the cream into a medium mixing bowl and beat on medium speed until thickened. Fold in the ricotta and then carefully fold in the chopped dark chocolate, pistachios, citron, cinnamon and clove oils, and vanilla. Pour the mixture into the large bowl with the ice cream and stir by hand to combine. Place the mixture in the freezer for at least 2 hours.

To make a tartufo, take one large scoop of the ice cream mixture, place a cherry in the center, and roll the ball in finely chopped dark chocolate. Repeat with the remaining ice cream. Freeze the tartufi for 2 to 3 hours.

Serve with whipped cream and fresh berries or serve on a bed of Salsa al Vin Cotto.

JASPER, JR.'S AFFOGATO

SERVES 4

Il Café was the name of my family's coffee shop when we were located in the Waldo neighborhood of Kansas City. This was one of my specialties there. I love to serve this to my friends because it is so simple to make, but very refreshing, light, and quintessentially Italian. It's made with gelato, an Italian ice cream. Like high-end ice cream, gelato generally has less than 55 percent air, resulting in a denser and more flavorful product than typical ice cream.

4 SMALL SCOOPS VANILLA GELATO

4 SHOTS FRESHLY BREWED HOT ESPRESSO COFFEE

COCOA POWDER, FOR DUSTING

4 MINT SPRIGS

4 BISCOTTI, FOR SERVING

Place a scoop of vanilla gelato into each of 4 cappuccino cups. Pour a shot of espresso over the gelato, dust the tops with cocoa, add a fresh mint sprig, and serve immediately with a biscotto.

PESCHE A VINO CHIANTI

SERVES 8

I can't recall a holiday without this dessert. My father would spend hours adjusting the recipe, adding mint, cinnamon sticks, cloves, and other flavorings. Sometimes we would serve it warm in the winter, but in the summer it was always chilled. It's also close to my heart because it was one of the desserts served at my wedding.

10 TO 12 FRESH PEACHES

1 CUP SUGAR

1 (750 ML) BOTTLE CHIANTI

1 QUART WHITE CHOCOLATE ICE CREAM

Boil a large pot of water, drop in the peaches, and let sit for about 10 seconds, then remove and slip off the skins. Cut each peach into 8 wedges. Place the wedges in a large bowl, sprinkle them with sugar, and let them sit for 1 hour. Add the Chianti and let sit for another 2 to 3 hours.

Divide the ice cream among 8 individual serving dishes, top with the macerated peaches, and drizzle the wine mixture over the top.

FLAMING BANANAS WITH GRAPPA

SERVES 6

If there is one after-dinner digestive that I enjoy, it has to be grappa! Grappa is everything left over after you make wine, including grapes, seeds, and skins. To cook with it—WOW, what flavor it adds. You will taste the perfume of the grape with a fiery finish.

6 TABLESPOONS (¾ STICK) UNSALTED BUTTER

1 CUP PACKED LIGHT BROWN SUGAR

6 RIPE BANANAS, PEELED, SLICED LENGTHWISE, AND HALVED

½ TEASPOON GROUND CINNAMON

¼ CUP BANANA LIQUEUR

½ CUP DARK RUM

¼ CUP GRAPPA

1 PINT VANILLA BEAN GELATO

Melt the butter in a large skillet over medium-low heat. Add the brown sugar and stir until the sugar dissolves completely, about 2 minutes.

Place the bananas in the pan and cook on both sides until they soften slightly and begin to brown, about 3 minutes. Sprinkle the cinnamon on top. Remove the pan from the heat and add the banana liqueur, rum, and grappa. Tip the pan slightly and carefully ignite the alcohol with a long kitchen match (or kitchen lighter) to flambé.

Return the pan to the heat and shake it back and forth to baste the bananas until the flame dies out.

Divide the gelato among individual dessert bowls. Gently lift the bananas from the pan and place the bananas on top of the gelato. Spoon the sauce over the gelato and serve immediately.

ZABAGLIONE

SERVES 2

This is a classic Italian dessert, and I love it because you can do so much with it. You can add cinnamon and grated lemon zest before pouring in the Marsala. You can replace the Marsala with a high-quality white, sweet, dry, or sparkling wine. You can even use brandy or cherry brandy. I encourage you to experiment with your own variations and find a combination you like.

3 EGG YOLKS

3 TABLESPOONS SUGAR

6 TABLESPOONS SWEET MARSALA WINE

FRESH SEASONAL BERRIES, FOR SERVING

Warm the egg yolks and sugar in a double boiler over hot water on low heat and then whip them with a wire whisk for 3 to 4 minutes, until frothy. Pour the Marsala into the egg yolks, drop by drop, beating continuously. The mixture will begin to foam and then swell into a light, soft cream. When it does so, immediately remove it from the heat. If you overcook it, it will collapse. Serve warm over fresh berries.

ESPRESSO CRÈME BRÛLÉE

SERVES 6

This is a great dessert for friends and company, and as a special touch I use a mini-blowtorch to caramelize the sugar in front of everyone. If you don't like espresso, just omit it. You'll still have a nice chocolate crème brûlée.

2 CUPS HEAVY CREAM

1 TABLESPOON INSTANT ESPRESSO POWDER

5 OUNCES BITTERSWEET CHOCOLATE, CHOPPED

6 EGG YOLKS

3 TABLESPOONS PLUS ¼ CUP SUGAR

1 TEASPOON PURE VANILLA EXTRACT

FRESH MINT, FOR GARNISH

CHOCOLATE-COVERED ESPRESSO BEANS, FOR GARNISH

Preheat the oven to 300°F. In a medium saucepan, combine the cream and espresso powder and bring to a simmer, whisking to dissolve the espresso powder. Remove the mixture from the heat, add the chocolate, and whisk until smooth. Set aside.

In a large mixing bowl, whisk the egg yolks, 3 tablespoons of the sugar, and the vanilla until well blended. Gradually whisk in the chocolate mixture. Strain into a clean bowl, skimming off any foam or bubbles. Divide the mixture among 6 four-ounce ramekins. Place the ramekins in a 9 by 13-inch baking dish and pour hot water into the baking dish until it comes halfway up the sides of the ramekins. Carefully place the baking dish in the oven and bake until the custards are set around the edges but still loose in the center, 40 to 50 minutes. Remove from the oven and leave the ramekins in the water bath until cooled.

The custards can be served warm or chilled. To chill, refrigerate for at least 2 hours or up to 2 days. When ready to serve, sprinkle about 2 teaspoons of the sugar over each of the custards. For best results, use a small chef's torch to melt the sugar. If you don't have a torch, place the ramekins on a baking sheet and place them under the broiler until the sugar melts.

Serve garnished with fresh mint and chocolate-covered espresso beans.

PANNA COTTA AND MORELLO CHERRIES

SERVES 6

Panna cotta literally means "cooked cream." This simple but elegant dessert makes for a perfect ending to an authentic Italian meal. Morello cherries can be found in specialty stores and are packed in heavy syrup. The syrup can also be used to drizzle over the panna cotta!

1 CUP WHOLE MILK

1 TABLESPOON UNFLAVORED GELATIN POWDER

1 VANILLA BEAN

3 CUPS HEAVY CREAM

⅓ CUP HONEY

1 TABLESPOON GRANULATED SUGAR

PINCH OF SALT

1 CUP MORELLO CHERRIES

Pour the milk into a small bowl and sprinkle the powdered gelatin on top. Let stand for 3 to 5 minutes to soften the gelatin. Pour the milk mixture into a heavy saucepan, add the vanilla bean, and cook over medium heat just until the gelatin dissolves but the milk does not boil, about 5 minutes.

Add the cream, honey, sugar, and salt. Stir until the sugar dissolves, 5 to 7 minutes. Remove the pan from the heat. Remove the vanilla bean and use a paring knife to split the bean in half lengthwise. Use the dull back of the paring knife to scrape the seeds into the pan. Stir to combine.

Pour the custard into 6 wineglasses, filling each about half full. Cool slightly for about 20 minutes, then refrigerate until set, at least 6 hours.

Spoon the Morello cherries on top of the panna cotta and serve.

JASPER'S TIRAMISU

SERVES 12

The classic Venetian dessert can be made with sponge cake instead of ladyfingers. You can also prepare it in a large bowl instead of a springform pan, lining the sides with ladyfingers or cake. Mascarpone is an Italian cream cheese that can be purchased at Italian specialty markets.

6 EGGS

1 CUP GRANULATED SUGAR

½ CUP CONFECTIONERS' SUGAR

2½ POUNDS MASCARPONE CHEESE

1 TABLESPOON ALMOND EXTRACT

¼ CUP AMARETTO

¼ CUP BRANDY

36 LADYFINGERS

3 CUPS BREWED AND COOLED ESPRESSO COFFEE

COCOA POWDER, FOR DUSTING

ESPRESSO BEANS OR CHOCOLATE-COVERED ESPRESSO BEANS, FOR GARNISH

Bring a saucepan of water to a boil, remove from the heat, and add the eggs. Let sit for 2 minutes, then remove the eggs, separate them, and discard the whites. In a mixing bowl, whip the granulated sugar, confectioners' sugar, and the coddled egg yolks on medium speed until blended. Add the mascarpone, almond extract, amaretto, and brandy and beat until fluffy, 3 to 5 minutes.

Line a 10-inch springform pan with plastic wrap and spread about a third of the cheese mixture on the bottom. Dip the ladyfingers in the espresso one at a time and arrange them in a layer on top of the cheese mixture. Add another third of the cheese mixture and dust it with a little cocoa powder. Repeat that process for the remaining layers. Refrigerate the tiramisu overnight.

To serve, loosen the ring from the springform pan and carefully invert the pan onto a serving plate so that the bottom becomes the top. Peel away and discard the plastic wrap. Decorate the tiramisu with espresso beans or chocolate-covered espresso beans.

CRUNCHY AMARETTO TIRAMISU

SERVES 8

Tiramisu is one of the most popular and widely consumed Italian desserts, and I think you'll really enjoy this twist on the classic version.

8 OUNCES MASCARPONE CHEESE,
  AT ROOM TEMPERATURE

⅓ CUP GRANULATED SUGAR

¼ CUP PLUS 2 TABLESPOONS AMARETTO
  LIQUEUR

½ TEASPOON VANILLA EXTRACT

3 CUPS FRESHLY WHIPPED CREAM

24 LADYFINGERS

¾ CUP BREWED AND COOLED
  ESPRESSO COFFEE

2½ CUPS COCOA POWDER

CONFECTIONERS' SUGAR, FOR DUSTING

1 CUP CRUSHED AMARETTI COOKIES,
  FOR GARNISH

In a medium mixing bowl, combine the mascarpone and sugar. Beat with a mixer on medium speed until light and creamy, 3 to 4 minutes. While continuing to beat the mixture, add the amaretto and vanilla. Fold in the whipped cream.

Arrange half of the ladyfingers in a layer across the bottom of a 9-inch square glass baking dish. Sprinkle with half of the coffee and spread half of the mascarpone mixture smoothly over the top. Sprinkle with half of the cocoa. Arrange the remaining ladyfingers over the cocoa, sprinkle with the remaining coffee, and top with a smooth layer of the remaining mascarpone mixture. Sprinkle with the remaining cocoa.

Cover and refrigerate for at least 4 hours, preferably overnight. Dust the top with confectioners' sugar and sprinkle with crushed amaretti before serving.

LIMONCELLO CAKE

SERVES 8

My friend and customer Bonnie Knocke loves limoncello, and one day, before dinner service, Bonnie brought in this cake in the process of developing the recipe for Jasper's. I swear I must have eaten the whole cake—I don't remember! Grazie mille, Bonnie!

CAKE

- 1 (18.25-OUNCE) BOX YELLOW CAKE MIX
- 1 (4.3-OUNCE) BOX INSTANT VANILLA PUDDING MIX
- ½ CUP CORN OIL
- ¼ CUP WATER
- ¾ CUP LIMONCELLO
- 4 WHOLE EGGS PLUS 1 EGG YOLK
- ¼ CUP GRATED LEMON ZEST

GLAZE

- ¾ CUP PACKED BROWN SUGAR
- 12 TABLESPOONS (1½ STICKS) BUTTER
- ½ CUP LIMONCELLO
- 3 TABLESPOONS FRESHLY SQUEEZED LEMON JUICE
- 3 TABLESPOONS GRATED LEMON ZEST

Preheat the oven to 325°F and grease a Bundt pan.

Combine all the ingredients for the cake in a large mixing bowl and mix well. Pour the mixture into the prepared Bundt pan and bake for 1 hour, or until golden brown and a toothpick inserted in the center of the cake comes out clean.

While the cake is baking, prepare the glaze. Combine all the glaze ingredients in a medium saucepan and bring to a boil over medium-high heat, stirring constantly. Cook for about 4 minutes to a creamy consistency.

Remove the cake from the oven, invert it onto a serving plate, and poke holes in the top. Remove the glaze mixture from the stove and immediately pour the hot glaze over the cake.

Let the cake cool for 1 hour before serving.

Limoncello is made from three basic ingredients: lemon, sugar, and pure alcohol. It captures the spirit of the Italian lifestyle in a glass. Visitors to Italy will tell you about the abundance of lemon groves that trail down the Amalfi coast, wrapping around towns such as Capri and Sorrento. This is where the limoncello tradition was born.

VIN SANTO AND OLIVE OIL CAKE

SERVES 8 TO 10

When I first traveled to Italy as a child, I discovered "olive oil cakes." The flavor is outstanding. I recommend you enjoy it with Vin Santo wine. The marriage of flavors makes for a rare taste of sweet wine and olives.

1 CUP ALL-PURPOSE FLOUR

½ TEASPOON SALT

5 LARGE EGGS, SEPARATED, PLUS 2 LARGE EGG WHITES

½ CUP GRANULATED SUGAR

2 TABLESPOONS GRATED LEMON ZEST, OR MORE TO TASTE

½ CUP VIN SANTO WINE

½ CUP EXTRA VIRGIN OLIVE OIL

1 PINT FRESH BERRIES, PLUS BERRIES FOR GARNISH

2 TO 4 TABLESPOONS CONFECTIONERS' SUGAR

Preheat the oven to 325°F. Brush a 10-inch round cake pan with vegetable oil.

Whisk together the flour and salt in a medium bowl and set aside.

In a large bowl, beat the 5 egg yolks with the granulated sugar on medium-high speed for 2 to 3 minutes, until the mixture is light yellow and ribbons form when you lift the beaters. Add the flour mixture to the egg yolk mixture and beat on medium-low speed until well blended. Beat in the lemon zest until combined.

Combine the wine and olive oil in a small bowl and gradually pour it into the egg yolk mixture in a thin, steady stream, beating until thoroughly combined. Set aside.

In a clean mixing bowl, beat the 7 egg whites until stiff but dry peaks do not form. Use a rubber spatula to gently fold a third of the whites into the egg yolk mixture, then gently fold in the remaining whites just until combined.

Pour the batter into the prepared pan. Bake for 45 to 50 minutes, or until the cake springs back when touched gently and a toothpick inserted in the center comes out clean. Remove the pan from the oven and cool on a wire rack. Run a thin knife along the edge of the pan, then loosen the ring and carefully transfer the cake to a serving platter.

In a blender or food processor, pulse the berries and confectioners' sugar until smooth, about 30 seconds. Top the cake with the purée and garnish with whole fresh berries.

CLASSIC TORINO CHOCOLATE LAVA CAKES

SERVES 4

A few years ago, I visited Torino with my Slow Food Convivium and fell in love with the chocolate. Actually, I became obsessed with it! This dish looks difficult to make, but it is really quite simple. You can use either bittersweet or semisweet chocolate, but I don't recommend unsweetened chocolate—no matter how bitter you like your chocolate.

6½ OUNCES BITTERSWEET OR SEMISWEET
   CHOCOLATE, CHOPPED

3 TABLESPOONS UNSALTED BUTTER

PINCH OF SALT

2 WHOLE LARGE EGGS, SEPARATED,
   PLUS 2 EGG YOLKS

¼ CUP SUGAR

ESPRESSO CREAM SAUCE, FOR SERVING
   (RECIPE FOLLOWS)

WHIPPED CREAM, FOR SERVING (OPTIONAL)

Preheat the oven to 425°F. Butter four 6-ounce custard cups, dust with flour, and shake out the excess.

Combine the chocolate, butter, and salt in the top of a double boiler set over simmering water. Stir until the chocolate is melted and the mixture is smooth. Remove the top of the double boiler from the bottom and cool for 10 minutes.

Meanwhile, use an electric mixer to beat the egg yolks and 3 tablespoons of the sugar in a large bowl on medium-high speed until thick and light, about 2 minutes. Use a rubber spatula to fold in the chocolate mixture.

In a clean medium bowl, using an electric mixer fitted with clean, dry beaters, beat the egg whites with the remaining tablespoon of sugar until stiff but dry peaks do not form. Gently fold the whites into the chocolate mixture in 3 equal portions, each time mixing just until the whites are incorporated.

Divide the batter among the prepared custard cups. Place the custard cups on a baking sheet and bake until the cakes are puffed out but still soft in the center, about 11 minutes. Transfer the baking sheet to a rack and cool for about 3 minutes.

Using a small, thin knife, cut around the sides of the cakes to loosen them from the cups. Place individual serving plates on top of each cup and invert each cake onto a plate. Remove the cups.

Spoon the Espresso Cream Sauce around the cakes and top each cake with whipped cream, if using.

ESPRESSO CREAM SAUCE

MAKES 1 1/2 CUPS

This delicious coffee-flavored sauce is the perfect accompaniment to chocolate desserts. A dollop of sauce, fresh berries, a chocolate dessert, and you're in culinary heaven!

3 LARGE EGG YOLKS

¼ CUP SUGAR

1 CUP HEAVY CREAM

1 TEASPOON INSTANT ESPRESSO POWDER

1 ½ TEASPOONS COARSELY GROUND ESPRESSO BEANS

In a medium mixing bowl, beat the egg yolks and sugar on medium speed until thick and light yellow, about 2 minutes.

In a heavy medium saucepan, bring the cream to a simmer over medium-high heat. Gradually whisk the hot cream into the egg yolk mixture, then return the mixture to the same saucepan. Stir over medium-low heat until the sauce thickens and leaves a path on the back of a spoon when a finger is drawn across it, about 3 minutes. Do not allow the mixture to boil.

Strain the mixture into a clean medium bowl, add the espresso powder, and stir until dissolved. Stir in the ground espresso beans.

Refrigerate the sauce until cold, whisking occasionally, about 1 hour.

JASPER'S ESPRESSO AND CHOCOLATE TORTE

SERVES 8

I use a springform pan and let this torte cool completely in the pan. I also serve this with white chocolate gelato. Delicious!

5 OUNCES SEMISWEET CHOCOLATE, CHOPPED

3 OUNCES UNSWEETENED CHOCOLATE, CHOPPED

8 TABLESPOONS (1 STICK) BUTTER

4 EGGS, AT ROOM TEMPERATURE

½ CUP SUGAR

¼ CUP BREWED ESPRESSO,
 COOLED TO ROOM TEMPERATURE

1 TABLESPOON FINELY GROUND
 ESPRESSO BEANS

PINCH OF SALT

¼ CUP ALL-PURPOSE FLOUR

Preheat the oven to 350°F. Butter an 8-inch cake pan (I prefer springform) and line the bottom with a round of parchment paper. Lightly dust the pan with a little flour or cocoa powder and shake out any excess.

In a heavy small saucepan, melt the chocolates and butter over medium heat, stirring frequently. Set aside.

Using the whisk attachment of a stand mixer, whip the eggs, sugar, brewed espresso, ground espresso beans, and salt on medium-high speed until thick and voluminous, at least 8 to 10 minutes. Turn the mixer to low and mix in the chocolate mixture. Turn off the mixer, sift the flour over the batter, and use a rubber spatula to fold the batter until fully incorporated.

Pour the batter into the prepared pan and bake until a skewer inserted into the center comes out clean, 25 to 30 minutes.

Cool the torte in the pan on a rack for 10 minutes. Set a plate on top of the pan and carefully invert the torte onto the plate. Peel off the parchment, then flip the torte back onto the rack to cool completely before transferring it to a serving plate and slicing.

JASPER'S CASSATA ALLA SICILIANA
SERVES 8 TO 10

This is one of the classics among Sicilian cakes. It was originally a lavish Holy Week sponge cake, made exclusively by the nuns.

1 ¼ POUNDS RICOTTA CHEESE

2 CUPS CONFECTIONERS' SUGAR, PLUS MORE FOR DUSTING

1 DROP CINNAMON OIL

1 (4-OUNCE) DARK CHOCOLATE ALMOND BAR, CHOPPED

¼ CUP CANDIED FRUITS (CANDIED LEMONS, ORANGES, AND CHERRIES)

¼ CUP CHOPPED PISTACHIO OR PINE NUTS

1 POUND SPONGE CAKE

5 TABLESPOONS MARASCHINO CHERRY LIQUEUR

In a large bowl, beat the ricotta cheese until smooth, 3 minutes at medium speed. In a medium saucepan over low heat, dissolve the confectioners' sugar in 2 to 3 tablespoons of water. Immediately remove the pan from the heat and beat the sugar mixture into the ricotta.

Add a drop of cinnamon oil and the chopped chocolate and mix well. Divide the candied fruits in half, reserving the best pieces to decorate the cake, and chop the rest into very small pieces. Add the chopped candied fruit and the nuts to the ricotta mixture and mix well.

Cut the sponge cake into ½-inch-thick slices and moisten them with the maraschino cherry liqueur. Line a deep round bowl about 10 inches in diameter with some of the slices of cake and add a layer of the ricotta cheese mixture on top, smoothing it down neatly with the blade of a knife. Cover with the remaining slices of sponge cake and chill in the refrigerator for several hours, preferably overnight.

Cut a cardboard base the same size as the top of the mixing bowl and cover it with a round of wax paper. Place it on top of the bowl with the wax paper side toward the cake. Holding the cardboard base firmly over the bowl, turn the bowl upside down and carefully lift the bowl off the cake.

Decorate the cake with the reserved pieces of candied fruit (either whole or thickly sliced) and dust the top with sifted confectioners' sugar just before serving.

CROSTATA DI RICOTTA

SERVES 8 TO 10

Classic Sicilian—those two words describe this authentic dessert. When baked, the ricotta becomes light and airy, and the citrus imparts added pleasure to the palate.

CRUST

½ POUND (2 STICKS) BUTTER

½ CUP SUGAR

2 EGGS

3 CUPS ALL-PURPOSE FLOUR

PINCH OF SALT

FILLING

1 POUND RICOTTA CHEESE

1 TABLESPOON ALL-PURPOSE FLOUR

1 CUP SUGAR

2 TABLESPOONS FRESHLY SQUEEZED ORANGE JUICE

4 EGGS

FRESH BERRIES, FOR SERVING

WHIPPED CREAM, FOR SERVING

Preheat the oven to 400°F.

To make the crust, cream the butter and sugar together using an electric mixer. Add the eggs and mix at low speed until well combined. Stir in the flour and salt just until incorporated.

Roll out the dough on a lightly floured work surface until the dough is about ⅛ inch thick. Transfer the dough to a greased 8-inch tart pan. Place a piece of aluminum foil over the dough and fill the tart shell with dried beans or pie weights. Bake for 12 to 15 minutes.

Remove the pan from the oven, lift out the foil and the pie weights, and cool the crust completely on a wire rack.

Reduce the oven temperature to 350°F.

To make the filling, combine the ricotta, flour, sugar, orange juice, and eggs in a large mixing bowl and mix well. Turn the filling into the cooled tart crust. Bake for 25 minutes, or until light golden brown.

Cool the tart on a wire rack. Decorate with fresh berries and whipped cream and serve.

Jasper III's Blood Orange Candy

Serves 12 to 15

My nephew Jasper returned from Sicily with many new ideas and a new appreciation for Sicilian cuisine and our family in Gibellina. We have been sampling some old recipes from Sicily, including many for pasta, but the best by far is this recipe for candied Sicilian blood orange slices.

2 BLOOD ORANGES

1 CUP SUGAR

Preheat the oven to 350°F.

Slice the oranges paper-thin. Dip the slices in sugar and place them on baking sheets. Bake for 20 minutes, until crisp. Remove the pan from the oven and place it on a rack to dry for at least 2 days before serving. The candy can be stored in an airtight container for several weeks.

Cousin Reno's Granita

Serves 6 to 8

Reno is my cousin from Sicily, and I am honored to have his recipe for granita. I have spent many vacations with Reno, which is short for Jasper. He is a master artisan gelato and granita maker. You will be in Sicily after one taste of this.

9 LEMONS, HALVED

1 QUART WATER

2¼ CUPS GRANULATED SUGAR

BISCOTTI, FOR SERVING

SPRIGS OF FRESH MINT, FOR GARNISH

Squeeze the lemon juice into a large bowl. Add four of the lemon rinds and add the water to soak for about 5 minutes. Strain the water and the lemon juice and add the sugar. Dissolve the sugar for about 5 minutes.

Place the mixture in a 1-gallon ice cream freezer and freeze according to the manufacturer's directions.

Serve the granita with biscotti and a sprig of fresh mint.

MAMA'S SICILIAN SFINGE

SERVES 6

My nana and mom used to make these for me. These are the famous "doughnuts" of a Sicilian outdoor market called the Vucciria in Palermo, where street vendors sell them by the dozen in little brown paper sacks. Be careful—they are addictive!

1 CUP WATER

1 CUP ALL-PURPOSE FLOUR

DASH OF SALT

1 HEAPING TABLESPOON SOLID VEGETABLE SHORTENING

3 EGGS

CORN OIL, FOR DEEP-FRYING

CONFECTIONERS' SUGAR, FOR DUSTING

HONEY, FOR SERVING

Bring the water to a boil in a medium saucepan over high heat. When the water is boiling, remove the pan from the heat and add the flour, salt, and shortening. Beat well with a fork. Beat in the eggs one at a time.

Heat the oil to 350°F in a deep fryer. Spoon 1 tablespoon of the sfinge batter into the hot oil and fry until golden, 4 to 5 minutes. Drain on paper towels. Dust with the confectioners' sugar and drizzle the honey on top to serve.

LEMON MELTING MOMENTS

SERVES 8

This is my interpretation of the lemon bar, but with a twist. Grappa, the fiery, mysterious unaged brandy from Italy, is the by-product of the stems and skins left over from the winemaking process.

CRUST

½ POUND (2 STICKS) BUTTER

1⅓ CUPS ALL-PURPOSE FLOUR

¼ CUP GRANULATED SUGAR

FILLING

2 WHOLE EGGS

¾ CUP GRANULATED SUGAR

2 TABLESPOONS ALL-PURPOSE FLOUR

¼ TEASPOON VANILLA EXTRACT

3 TABLESPOONS FRESHLY SQUEEZED LEMON JUICE

LEMON SAUCE

8 TABLESPOONS (1 STICK) BUTTER

2 CUPS CONFECTIONERS' SUGAR

1 CUP FRESHLY SQUEEZED LEMON JUICE

1 TEASPOON VANILLA EXTRACT

¼ CUP GRAPPA

1 EGG, BEATEN

CONFECTIONERS' SUGAR, FOR SERVING

Preheat the oven to 350°F.

To make the crust, combine the butter, flour, and sugar in the bowl of a stand mixer and beat on medium speed until blended. Pat the dough into a 10-inch tart pan and bake for 15 to 18 minutes, or until golden brown.

To make the filling, combine the eggs, sugar, flour, vanilla, and lemon juice in a medium bowl and beat well. Pour the mixture into the crust. Return to the oven and bake for 18 to 20 minutes, or until lightly browned.

To make the lemon sauce, melt the butter in a medium saucepan over medium heat. Whisk in the confectioners' sugar and lemon juice and then add the vanilla and grappa. Finally, whisk in the egg until the mixture is smooth.

To serve, dust with the confectioners' sugar and serve plated on top of the lemon sauce.

CLASSIC SICILIAN CANNOLI

SERVES 6

This is definitely the most traditional and popular of all Sicilian desserts. My nephew and I once traveled through Italy in search of the perfect cannoli. You can read that story on page 150. Here's my favorite recipe. You can buy cannoli shells at Italian markets.

1 POUND RICOTTA CHEESE

1 CUP CONFECTIONERS' SUGAR, PLUS MORE FOR DUSTING

¼ CUP CANDIED ORANGES AND CHERRIES, DICED

¼ CUP CHOPPED DARK CHOCOLATE

2 DROPS CINNAMON OIL

6 CANNOLI SHELLS

Place the ricotta in a large mixing bowl and fold in the confectioners' sugar. Add the candied fruit, chocolate, and cinnamon oil and mix gently to combine. Refrigerate for 2 to 3 hours before serving.

To serve, fill the shells with the cheese mixture and dust them with confectioners' sugar.

PASTRY CUSTARD

MAKES 2 CUPS

Nana Josephine, as my mom is called today, makes this wonderful custard for Jasper's. We fill cream puffs, napoleons, and cakes with it, and we even serve it over fresh berries and top with toasted coconut. Grazie, Nanni!

5 EGG YOLKS

⅔ CUP SUGAR

⅓ CUP ALL-PURPOSE FLOUR

½ TEASPOON SALT

2 TEASPOONS VANILLA EXTRACT

2 CUPS SCALDING HOT MILK

1 TABLESPOON BUTTER

In a medium bowl, beat the egg yolks thoroughly for about 30 seconds. In a small bowl, whisk together the sugar, flour, salt, and vanilla, then beat the mixture into the egg yolks. Add the hot milk and cook, stirring constantly, in a double boiler over simmering water until thickened, 6 to 8 minutes. Remove from the heat, add the butter, and fold it into the custard. Chill for about 30 minutes before serving.

SALSA AL VIN COTTO

MAKES 2 CUPS

This is a great sauce to put on fresh berries, chilled desserts, melon, and poached pears. I also like to serve it with homemade gelato and biscotti.

3 CUPS CHIANTI

1 CUP GRANULATED SUGAR

4 TO 5 CLOVES

1 TO 2 CINNAMON STICKS

1 TABLESPOON GRATED ORANGE ZEST

2 TABLESPOONS BUTTER

In a large pot, combine the Chianti, sugar, cloves, cinnamon sticks, and orange zest. Bring the mixture to a boil, then add the butter and turn the heat to low. Cook, stirring, until the sauce thickens naturally, 10 to 15 minutes. Serve warm.

MEMORIES OF NANA MIRABILE'S KITCHEN

I was the youngest of four boys in the Mirabile family and spent a lot of time at my nana's. Who wouldn't? I had everything I wanted at her house—my own bicycle, toys, TV, and, of course, the attention of Nana!

Since my papa worked evenings with my grandfather at his restaurant, Nana was alone a lot, so she cooked for me many weekends. When other children in the neighborhood were playing baseball or hide and seek, I was in my nana's kitchen.

I remember all of her dishes, but some still hold a special place in my heart. One favorite was her Sunday Sauce (page 60), a recipe that is still used at Jasper's. Many of her other recipes remain on the menu at Jasper's today, but her Sunday Sauce was by far my favorite, with fragrant scents of garlic, fennel, basil, tomatoes, and just a hint of red pepper flakes. Wow! She put her meatballs and Italian sausage right in the pot, along with pork ribs and chicken. I was usually the first to sample the sauce before my brothers and parents arrived.

The next step in preparing for Nana's dinner was making homemade ravioli. She mixed her homemade ricotta cheese with freshly grated Romano cheese, fresh parsley, a hint of nutmeg, and a touch of salt. She also made her own pasta dough, using several eggs and flour, along with a touch of olive oil and a pinch of salt. She mixed the dough by hand and then rolled out the dough into thin sheets. I helped her fill a sheet with exactly 1 tablespoon of ricotta mixture per ravioli and then place another sheet of the golden-colored dough on top. Then we both held the rolling pin with the special cuts that formed the ravioli. The ravioli were laid out to dry on a sheet in the dining room, and I stared at them all day in anticipation of dinner! Nana always had a special treat for me for helping her in the kitchen. Was I spoiled, or what?

Such a learning experience could never be provided in school. Today, Nana's rolling pin sits on my desk as a little reminder of Nana. Each time I walk into my restaurant I can smell the sauce simmering on my stoves, and the memory of Nana and her favorite dish takes me back to a place I called home 40 years ago, Nana's kitchen.

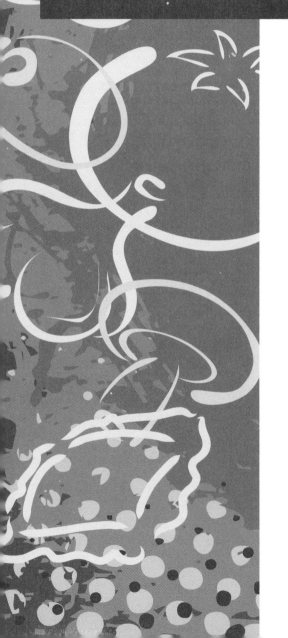

A LEGACY OF LOVE: THE LEGEND CONTINUES

My *father and mother were married in 1953.* They had four boys. Leonard is the oldest. Salvatore is the next oldest, and he's an attorney here in Kansas City. James is the next brother. He's an OB-GYN in Kansas City. And I, Jasper, am the youngest. Four boys in the family and no girls—you can imagine how that was growing up.

Today Leonard and I are partners at the restaurant, carrying on the tradition that my father started more than 55 years ago. We're fortunate that we have Leonard's son, my nephew Jasper III, working with us now and learning the same skills, doing the same work that we did growing up in the business.

When I was 8 years old, I cut bread at the restaurant, and my nephew started the same way. All the brothers started off in the kitchen when we were very young, working throughout the dining room, working with servers, working in the office, learning the bar. We have achieved the ultimate in cross-training—each of us can work any position in the restaurant! If a chef is sick one night, if a bartender is off, or if a hostess or one of our waiters is not at the restaurant, we've done it all, and we can fill in. That's what our family business is all about.

The generation that's coming into the family business today knows how hard we work. We haven't spent much time at home with our children, but that doesn't mean that we don't see them. My daughter and wife have dinner here at the restaurant at least four times a week. Leonard sees his children the same way, and they know what it's like growing up around the restaurant business.

We can't sit back and rest on our laurels, even after 55 years in business. We have to continue to grow and find new ways to please our customers. As I often say, "Tradition and authenticity for a new generation," that's what it's all about at Jasper's today. My nephew and I do extensive research to find new recipes and new dishes to serve our customers. We try to continually tweak the service a little bit and add special touches.

I think about my father and the way he did business, and he did BIG, BIG business back in the fifties. He put the money in a cigar box and paid his purveyors out of that box. Now we're taking reservations online and advertising differently, and things will continue to change. Many shy away from these changes, but for us it's a great learning experience, and it keeps us growing every day.

We really respect and appreciate all the awards that my father and our family have received over the years, but we can't rest on the success of the past. We have to keep going and growing every day to keep up with the changing times. However, we still have strong ties to our past, and we want to pass that on to our customers and keep pleasing them today.

ON THE CANNOLI TRAIL

Disclaimer: I bear no responsibility for weight gain, cravings, or other issues relating to cannoli.

More than a year ago, I planned to travel to Sicily with my Slow Food convivium from Kansas City, and I think that may have been where this whole cannoli issue started. We planned to arrive in Catania, visit the markets and restaurants, and learn about the local cuisine and the long history of Sicily.

I arrived on Monday with my nephew Jasper III and met our traveling companions. Our first stop was the ancient city of Siracusa, where I discovered pastry and gelato shops on every corner, much like Starbucks in the United States. I was going to pace myself and try to enjoy a cannoli a day but that was not going to work in Sicily!

After traveling for thirty hours, we were a little hungry to say the least, so before dinner we found a small restaurant that seated only twelve. The owner and her daughter were cooking; we asked for a plate of pasta because there was no menu Fifteen minutes later, they brought out a plate of spaghetti, steaming hot, tossed with fresh sardines, fennel, pine nuts, raisins, and olive oil, and topped with bread crumbs. From my childhood years visiting Sicily and my family's hometown of Gibellina, I knew this was pasta palermatana. It was cooked to perfection and tasted like it was prepared in someone's home. Actually, we were in someone's home—the outer kitchen and tables were an extension of the ladies' home.

Next, we went to a local osteria named da Mariano that my friend and local Italian guide, Judy Francini, found on a recent trip. We were greeted by the owner and chef, Mariano, who started us off with a Sicilian antipasto consisting of a homemade salame picante, eggplant caponata, a sauté of mushrooms and spinach, and a ricotta in pastry. He then sent out a course of three pastas: a spaghetti with sun-dried tomatoes, Sicilian olive oil, and pepperoncini; a pennette with local almonds, cream, and Pecorino cheese, dusted with ground almonds; and a fusilli tossed with a pesto of local greens and cheese. Our piatti del giorno followed with a lamb chop, arugula salad, and a piece of Sicilian fennel sausage. But the best was yet to come: a plate of orange sections drizzled with olive oil, red chiles, and Sicilian sea salt. Our wine was the local Nero d'Avola and dessert was a simple plate of candied ginger and sesame brittle but NO CANNOLO!

As we left the restaurant, I told my nephew we would have a cannoli on the walk back. But to our amazement, every place was closed but the gelaterias. Back at the Hotel Etrangers rooftop restaurant, the waiter also gave us the bad news: NO CANNOLO! I promised my nephew we would have one the following day.

On Wednesday morning, we awoke and went upstairs to an outrageous breakfast table consisting of over twenty pastries, some filled with ricotta cheese, some filled with pastry cream, and mini doughnuts to die for. Ah, the breakfast of Sicilians! We took a day trip back to Catania and the famous fish, meat, and produce market brought amazement to our group. Fishmongers were everywhere hawking their morning catch. I sampled a sea urchin "shot" well worth the 10 euros. Everyone should shoot a sea urchin once in their life! The produce looked like something out of an artist's studio—grapes the size of golf balls, lemons the color of limes, fresh figs and cactus pears, and on and on. There were also meat cases full of local cheeses and salumi, along with hanging goats and lamb.

After a drive to Taormina and a short tour, it was time for lunch. My nephew and I took off for Ristorante Maffei, off Via San Dominico, where we enjoyed fresh Veraci clams, grilled shrimp, and spaghetti alla Bottarga. Bottarga is tuna roe with a unique salty taste, and here it was simply tossed with extra virgin olive oil, shaved garlic, and Pachino tomatoes grown on the lava-laden soil of Mount Etna. Absolutely my favorite pasta in Sicily! For dessert, our first cannolo, a wine-scented crispy shell filled with light ricotta and a touch of cinnamon. On a scale of 1 to 10, I gave it an 8.5.

Later that afternoon, Jasper III and I searched for more cannolo. We made three more stops at local pastry and gelato shops, running on shots of espresso too many to count! Each cannolo was different in its own way—some filled with candied fruit, some dusted with local Bronte pistachios, and one filled with chocolate from Noto. At one stop, we really enjoyed an espresso freddo made with cane sugar, shaved ice, and heavy cream.

A few of the shops in Taormina even filled the cannolo with egg and vanilla pastry cream or gelato of your choice. A two-hour bus ride back to Siracusa gave us time to rest and savor more cannoli that we bought before leaving Taormina.

Back in Siracusa, we took a short rest before another evening of dining and cannoli searching. My nephew and I dined at Ristorante Castello Fiorentino, a famous pizzeria and ristorante owned by Riccioli Salvatore. We ordered a fresh calamari salad, zuppa di vongole, and a couple of pizzas, one topped with fresh mozzarella, anchovies, and sausage, the other wild mushrooms, fresh mozzarella, and prosciutto. After dinner, the owner offered us a refreshing lemon granita. I did not have the heart to ask for a cannolo, so we ventured back on the streets and went in a new direction, enjoying a cannolo from Antica Siciliano Dolceria that was very light with a flaky crust and another from a gelato shop near our hotel by the sea with a faint taste of sheep's milk and little sugar.

Thursday morning started with more pastry from the renowned pastry chef at Hotel Etrangers, some filled with mortadella, some with prosciutto, and most with sweet ricotta and pastry cream. All were served with cappuccino. Our tour for the day began with a one-hour bus ride to Noto, a small Baroque town in the southeast of Sicily to visit Café Sicilia, which has been owned by the same family since 1892. Today, the pastry shop holds on to its traditions, respecting the past but constantly updating desserts, offering wild combinations such as tart tomatoes and roasted

pepper dolce, along with combining fresh herbs and spices in ancient recipes. Some worked well, others did not. Corrado Assenza is considered the guru of international pastry. We listened as Corrado explained his modern interpretations of pastry, even explaining why he uses a light white wine for his cannolo. At that point, over an hour had passed and it was time to sample his cannolo, which were very heavily laden with sugar and had a distinct taste of fresh sheep's milk ricotta but no chocolate. I asked how he came up with this cannolo shell and he told me that he practiced making it 6 million times. He said this with a straight face.

A small lunch at a local Trattoria Giufa consisted of cavatelli alla Norma made with eggplant and tomatoes with shaved Pecorino, and cavatelli alla Mediterranean made with sun-dried tomatoes pureed and sautéed with capers from Pantelleria. A nice, refreshing salad of oranges, onions, and anchovies completed our tasting. A short espresso and we were back on the street.

Next, we stumbled on Café Noir, where we had cannoli dipped in chocolate and filled with sweet cream ricotta, which earned a 9.5 from this cannolo critic. Then it was on to Modica, a pleasant drive spent daydreaming and admiring cities built into the mountains, noticing wild vegetables and olive and orange groves close to the highway, all immaculately lined in rows. In Modica we visited the famous chocolate shop, Antica Dolceria Bonajuto. It is the oldest chocolate factory in Sicily and its chocolate is bittersweet and very grainy. We sampled the famous chocolate empanadas, brittle, torrone, orange slices, and, of course, chocolate. We also sampled some chocolate liqueur. Jasper III figured out the recipe, so we decided to feature it on our menu.

As our group walked the streets of the city, my nephew and I searched for a cannolo. It had been over an hour since our last cannolo, and I could not leave the city without one for the road! Just before we hopped on our bus, I discovered a pastry shop, where I had a piccolo cannolo, very small, just two bites but oh, so delicious—a good 9.0 rating. When we got to our hotel that night and I heard there was a gelateria next door that sells cannoli 24 hours a day, I thought, I HAVE DISCOVERED HEAVEN!

Next stop, Palermo, and a cooking school at Gangivecchio, and on to my family's hometown for gelato and granita and cannoli with my cousin Jasper. The three Jasper Mirabiles would be together for the first time. We took tours of salt pans, a Marsala factory, the 2008 olive oil press, had a nice luncheon at Olio Verde and, finally, paid a visit to the oldest pastry shop in Sicily, Maria Grammatico in Erice. Guess what I wanted for dessert?

After five more days of searching and eating cannoli, I finally discovered the greatest cannoli in the world, but I'm not ready to divulge it yet.

On Thursday evening, my nephew and I ate in a small trattoria in Siracusa named La Foglia. It was run by three women, so you can imagine how great the experience was. My father always told me that in every great Sicilian kitchen there is a woman cooking. We had a little pasta palermitana, a little pesce spada, a nice bottle of wine, and a cannolo to finish our dinner. That flaky pastry was crisp and bubbly, the filling firm and flavorful, but it was nothing to put on my trophy shelf so we ended up in a gelateria enjoying some creamy gelato and espresso despite the eleven o'clock hour.

The following morning, Jasper and I took a long walk over the bridge and bay into the actual city of Siracusa. There we stumbled upon a Sicilian market and poultry house that was roasting fresh young chickens and baking pans of pasta alla Norma. When in Sicily, you must eat, and we both agreed that for 14 euros it was a lunch of a lifetime—chicken encrusted with fresh rosemary and olive oil and roasted eggplant tossed with pasta. I wondered how I would manage a cannolo for dessert but around the corner and up the street was the most famous church in Siracusa, the Church of Mother Mary. It houses a statue of Mary that actually shed tears for four days in 1953—a twentieth-century miracle. Nearby, we found a pastry shop with a lady in her early nineties filling cannolo to order. Her name was Madonna, which seemed like a sign that a great cannolo was to be enjoyed there near the site where the miracle happened. The cannolo was hard and crisp, the filling stiff and flavorful, but it was not what I was searching for. We walked five miles back to our hotel and rested before our final evening with our group in Siracusa, where we would dine at Don Camillo, owned by Chiuso Domenica.

Dinner started with a raw oyster and lime followed by a crispy squid ink fried shrimp floating in a small bowl of almond soup. Then risotto and sea urchins and a small taste of fusilli pasta tossed with fresh tomatoes, fresh tuna, garlic, and mint. Two seafood courses and a few hours later, we enjoyed a taste of Cassata Siciliano, a marzipan iced cake soaked with liqueur and layered with cannolo filling. After traveling to Sicily since I was eight years old, this was definitely the best cassata that I have ever tasted.

On Saturday morning, our adventure started on a bus ride through the mountains by Mount Etna, and we were off to discover new friends in Gangivecchio. We arrived at the hilltop town and were greeted with open arms by famiglia from Kansas City. There we were at the farmhouse, villa, and cooking school, touring the grounds of the fourteenth-century abbey in the Madonie Mountains. Mr. and Mrs. Sacamano introduced us to the owner, Giovanna Tornabene, and our cooking class began. We learned to make a special pizza dough and baked pasta dish similar to a timpano. She finished the lesson with a recipe for her family's cannoli and she actually told us her secret for a crisp shell: red wine vinegar aged in the abbey. The cooking class was followed by a walk through the garden and abbey, into an upstairs dining room overlooking a breathtaking view of the mountains. There we feasted on the antipasti of warm ricotta, local olives, caponata, and pizza, followed by the delicious baked pasta and cannolo. Giovanna was correct—her cannoli was by far the finest we have enjoyed, the ricotta made fresh that morning from local sheep's milk. The Sacamanos were our personal hosts and we talked for hours about family, their efforts to start a trail on the farm, life in Sicily, and, of course, food. After dinner, Giovanna signed copies of her three James Beard Award–winning cookbooks, and a tour of the olive mill and frescos in the abbey concluded our day full of memories, followed by a sad good-bye with hugs and kisses from our newfound friends.

A two-hour ride to Palermo and our Hotel Excelsior Palace was quiet and peaceful, a time to rest before our next five days of excursions on the west coast and to my family's hometown. Jasper and I walked a few miles through the streets of Palermo in search of Piazza Olivella, hidden from tourists. It is in Palermo's outdoor trattoria district, with over fifteen restaurants on a small street, all offering antipasti, pizza, and pasta. We ordered a pizza and local vino, and watched the crowd of local teenagers and adults go from bar to bar, grabbing a bite to eat, talking on their cell phones, and drinking beer. As we walked to our hotel I spotted a large gelateria and lo and behold a display case with cannoli. I ordered a small one and at that point my nephew confirmed that I was indeed crazy, and wondered out loud when I would stop with the cannoli. I explained again that it was for research, and we must continue until we find the best. Little did I know what lay ahead.

A 7:00 a.m. phone call from my cousin Reno (Jasper Mirabile from Gibellina, Sicily) started our day. As the elevator door opened, he was waiting with tears in his eyes. His only cousins in America had returned for a visit. For the next four days all three remaining Jasper Mirabiles were finally together. Not since 1983 when Reno visited Kansas City had all the Jasper's been together. A picture in my office at Jasper's displays Jasper Mirabile, Sr., my father, myself, my nephew, and Jasper from Gibellina.

We left Palermo for Gibellina, a short forty-five-minute ride full of conversation. I speak very little Sicilian and Reno speaks very little English, but our conversation never stopped. And as Reno drove 145 kilometers an hour through the mountains, we held on until the final turn off A 29 and the road to Gibellina. We immediately went across the street to his coffee shop and gelateria where friends and cousins were waiting. Many of my father and grandfather's friends came to see us. We immediately had a short lesson in granita making, as this was why we actually traveled to see Reno, who is known throughout Provincia Trapani as "the Best Granita Maker." People drive from small towns all around Sicily to savor his granita. But first, it was Sunday noontime and that meant it was time to eat—and did we ever eat. Reno had an antipasti on the kitchen table with local provolone, salami, home-cured olives, and sun-dried tomatoes, black bread from Castelvetrano and my favorite, pasta alla Casa, a fresh tomato sauce laden with Sicilian fennel sausage, another family tradition, along with fresh pieces of pork, filled eggplant rolls, and frittata.

Then Reno brought out three trays. He uncovered the first with a smile, a tray of pignalotti, cookies shaped like pinecones soaked with honey made locally by friends of my father. Next came Cassatete, a small half-moon pastry filled with ricotta and fried oh-so-delicately made by another cousin. I thought of me and my father the last time we ate together at the same table in Gibellina. I went over to the sofa, closed my eyes, and fell asleep. I dreamt of my family at home, my father, and life in Sicily. I awoke and everyone was back across the street watching soccer at my cousin's shop, enjoying granita and espresso.

Jasper and I spent the rest of the day learning the secret of granita. As Reno told me many times, I could write the recipe down, you can buy the best machine from Bologna, but it was all in his head. He kept pointing to his head, telling me you must remember this and you must do this to carry on the tradition. Reno is sixty years old and in August of 2009, he will be selling the gelateria and coffee shop and retiring. I asked if he was giving the recipe with the sale, and he laughed and said, "It is just water, lemons, and sugar" but only you know the secret—it is in your head. I treasure that moment and I will always remember his words. Our grandfathers would be proud of the passing of a tradition from one family member to another.

On Monday we traveled to Castelvetrano to Olio Verde where we watched the 2008 olive oil harvest and the first pressing of what experts agree is the finest olive oil in Sicily. We met the owners, the Becchina family. After a one-hour cooking class, we enjoyed a beautiful luncheon of fresh ricotta and assorted marmalades, Pane Nero di Castelvetrano drenched with Olio Verde, Sicilian pesto made with fresh almonds, basil, Pecorino, and Olio Verde 2008, bracioline (oil-soaked bread, mortadella, and provolone-filled beef rolls), and a classic dessert, Torta all'olio d'oliva (olive oil cake). Everyone purchased bottles of the new oil, packed right in front of us. I was sad we had no cannoli, but I was anxious to take my group to visit Gibellina. We arrived in the small town and everyone was there to greet us. My cousin was waiting with a big smile, so proud that his family from America was bringing a group. He had eight types of gelato along with his homemade granita. We all stood around, talked, and sampled biscotti. What a perfect ending to a great day, or so I thought.

As the bus left, Reno informed Jasper III and myself that we were going to see the ruins of Selinunte and have dinner by the sea. Wow, just what we needed! We watched some soccer for a while, closed up the café, and off we went to a little restaurant that my papa used to eat at, but not before a quick stop to see some cousins. We finally arrived at Pietro and enjoyed small plates of pasta Trapani, swordfish, and grilled prawns. For dessert, take a guess. Just let me put it this way: It was very good, a 9.2 on my scale. We traveled back to Casa Mirabile to spend the evening and onto Marsala the next morning.

Reno drove us to meet our group in Marsala, where I had set up a tour at the famous Florio, and what a tour we had! My friend Bill Whiting from Banfi made the contact and we had a private walk through the cellars, a history of Marsala, and a lunch and tasting of arancine (Sicilian rice balls), sfincone (Sicilian pizza), panini, and the many flights of Marsala, another afternoon to cherish. And, of course, we sampled cannoli, and they were also great. The cannoli just kept getting better!

We left Marsala and traveled to the Infersa Saltworks where we watched a short film on the history of salt production and toured an ancient windmill still in use today for salt production. Sorry, no cannolo on this stop, but we did travel on for dinner to an old farmhouse, Baglio Elena Azienda Agrituristica Mezzo Sole, where we met Pietre Tagliate, a famous Italian comedian and movie star and now sculptor. His family cooked us a dinner of couscous, an ancient Arab dish of grains and brodo to finish. For dessert, cannolo and fried pastries, and we were on the way to Erice in the mountains. There we visited Maria Grammatico, one of the most important pastry chefs in Sicily who was taught her trade by nuns at a convent where she was raised. Just Google her name and see why her establishment is a mecca for chefs from around the world. Our guide, Judy Francini, convinced Maria to give us her cannolo shell recipe and sure enough, she uses red wine vinegar and old red wine. Another recipe, another day in Sicilia. By the way, Maria's cannoli were perfecto—the best shell so far, and a nice 9.6.

Next we traveled to the Capo market where we sampled spleen sandwiches, met many of the vendors, and walked the streets of Palermo, tasting cookies, salami, cheeses, and olives. My nephew and I snuck off to a small pastry shop at the end of the mercato and enjoyed another cannolo (are you keeping count?), but none as good as the cannolo in Gibellina. Next we ate a late lunch at Monsu where we sampled tripe, cow's mouth and cheeks, veal stew, and caponata. Jasper and I threw in the towel and said it was time to go back to the hotel. While in the cab, I remembered Spinnato, the most famous pastry shop in Palermo, which was near our hotel. I convinced the cab driver to wait while Jasper and I sampled the famous Torta de Sette Veili, a seven-layer sinful chocolate cake. OUTSTANDING is all I can say—and so delicate. We had to sample the cannolo, which were bite size and very sweet, laden with candied fruit and Bronte Pistaccio. Not the best, but oh so close.

For dinner, my cousin traveled back to Palermo with us, where we dined at Ristorante Cin Cin, owned by Vincenzo Clemente and his mother from Corleone, Sicily. We have much in common because my mother's famiglia is from Corleone. Vincenzo and his mama made us caponata baroque, an ancient eggplant recipe containing caramelized onions, eggplant, almonds, currents, and tiny squid—maybe the best sampled so far—along with finely chopped and grilled mussels served on lemon leaves. A rich and creamy risotto with fennel, shrimp, and asparagus followed, along with an involtini of swordfish filled with an orange, pistachio, and mint pesto drizzled with olio verde and sautéed cherry tomatoes from Corleone. After dinner, we

toasted our friends, one another, and my cousin Reno, and we all promised to meet again for a reunion at Jasper's.

For Jasper and I, it was a sad walk to my cousin's car where hugs and kisses and a promise to return ended our time in Palermo. Too little time, and so far away in another country, and all we have are memories. My nephew and I walked back to the hotel, both looking the other way when Reno drove by, hiding our tears but cherishing our memories of our Sicilian heritage.

In our hotel lobby, the front desk clerk called out, "Mr. Mirabile, I have a package for you." We ran to the desk and there was a package from Cousin Reno. He had left it at the desk with instructions to give it to us after he left. Jasper and I raced back to our room and unwrapped the package. There in front of us were six cannoli. Tears came to my eyes again. Jasper and I sat back, took a deep breath, and took our first bite of Reno's cannolo. I savored the sheep's ricotta, the hints of cinnamon, bits of chocolate all filled into a delicate shell lightly fried, crispy and topped with powdered sugar. Now this was heaven. This was IT—the best cannolo, hands down. A perfect 10! It took ten days and forty-three cannoli to find it. I was five thousand miles from home and ended up finding the best cannolo at my family's home in Gibellina. I took another bite and thought of Reno. No more research; I was done. *Fini.* Salute Cousin Reno! Salute Sicily! Salute cannoli!

About the Chef

Jasper J. Mirabile, Jr., was named executive chef of Jasper's in May of 1984, at the young age of 22. He had spent his college years at the University of Nevada, Las Vegas, Hotel and Restaurant School. During the summer vacations each year he would travel to Europe to visit cooking schools in Paris, Venice, and Milan. He was the first chef from Kansas City to be invited to the prestigious James Beard House in New York City, where he received rave reviews and was recognized by the foundation for his outstanding efforts to uphold the tradition of authentic Italian cuisine.

Today Jasper, Jr., oversees the kitchen staff, creating regional Italian cuisine and seasonal menus. He can be found many nights working the stoves and dining rooms, offering tips to his customers and assistants. Jasper, Jr., travels extensively throughout Italy each year, researching new restaurants, attending cooking classes, touring wineries and visiting small producers for Italian products.

Jasper currently teaches cooking classes and is co-chairman of the American Institute for Food and Wine; Vice Charge de Missions Honoraire Chaîne des Rôtisseurs; Convivium leader of Slow Food Kansas City; National Board Member of Gruppo Ristoratori Italiani; and Wisconsin Cheese Ambassador.

For additional information about Jasper, Jr., and Jasper's Restaurant, please visit his Web site at www.jasperskc.com.

Awards and Press

Past recognition includes:
"Best Italian Restaurant in Kansas City"
Zagat

"Top Ten Italian Restaurant in America"
East-West Network

"Distinguished Restaurants of North America"
DiRoNA Award

"Most Satisfying Dish of the Year"
USA Today

"Four Stars"
Kansas City Star

"Four Diamonds"
AAA

"One of America's Most Honored Restaurants"
Bob Lape, WCBS Radio, New York City

"A Culinary Delight"
Rave reviews for the first chef from Kansas City invited to the prestigious James Beard House

"Silver Spoon Award"
Ingram's magazine

"The Return of Jasper's Is the Best Gift for Local Gastronomes"
Art Simmering, *Kansas City Star* food critic

"An Italian Restaurant in the Middle of an Oasis"
Luige Veronelli, famous Italian food critic
Ambassador 25 Award

METRIC CONVERSIONS AND EQUIVALENTS

METRIC CONVERSION FORMULAS

To Convert	Multiply
Ounces to grams	Ounces by 28.35
Pounds to kilograms	Pounds by .454
Teaspoons to milliliters	Teaspoons by 4.93
Tablespoons to milliliters	Tablespoons by 14.79
Fluid ounces to milliliters	Fluid ounces by 29.57
Cups to milliliters	Cups by 236.59
Cups to liters	Cups by .236
Pints to liters	Pints by .473
Quarts to liters	Quarts by .946
Gallons to liters	Gallons by 3.785
Inches to centimeters	Inches by 2.54

APPROXIMATE METRIC EQUIVALENTS

Volume

1/4 teaspoon	1 milliliter
1/2 teaspoon	2.5 milliliters
3/4 teaspoon	4 milliliters
1 teaspoon	5 milliliters
1 1/4 teaspoon	6 milliliters
1 1/2 teaspoon	7.5 milliliters
1 3/4 teaspoon	8.5 milliliters
2 teaspoons	10 milliliters
1 tablespoon (1/2 fluid ounce)	15 milliliters
2 tablespoons (1 fluid ounce)	30 milliliters
1/4 cup	60 milliliters
1/3 cup	80 milliliters
1/2 cup (4 fluid ounces)	120 milliliters
2/3 cup	160 milliliters
3/4 cup	180 milliliters
1 cup (8 fluid ounces)	240 milliliters
1 1/4 cups	300 milliliters
1 1/2 cups (12 fluid ounces)	360 milliliters
1 2/3 cups	400 milliliters
2 cups (1 pint)	460 milliliters
3 cups	700 milliliters
4 cups (1 quart)	0.95 liter
1 quart plus 1/4 cup	1 liter
4 quarts (1 gallon)	3.8 liters

Weight

1/4 ounce	7 grams
1/2 ounce	14 grams
3/4 ounce	21 grams
1 ounce	28 grams
1 1/4 ounces	35 grams
1 1/2 ounces	42.5 grams
1 2/3 ounces	45 grams
2 ounces	57 grams
3 ounces	85 grams
4 ounces (1/4 pound)	113 grams
5 ounces	142 grams
6 ounces	170 grams
7 ounces	198 grams
8 ounces (1/2 pound)	227 grams
16 ounces (1 pound)	454 grams
35.25 ounces (2.2 pounds)	1 kilogram

Length

1/8 inch	3 millimeters
1/4 inch	6 millimeters
1/2 inch	1 1/4 centimeters
1 inch	2 1/2 centimeters
2 inches	5 centimeters
2 1/2 inches	6 centimeters
4 inches	10 centimeters
5 inches	13 centimeters
6 inches	15 1/4 centimeters
12 inches (1 foot)	30 centimeters

OVEN TEMPERATURES

To convert Fahrenheit to Celsius, subtract 32 from Fahrenheit, multiply the result by 5, then divide by 9.

Description	Fahrenheit	Celsius	British Gas Mark
Very cool	200°	95°	0
Very cool	225°	110°	1/4
Very cool	250°	120°	1/2
Cool	275°	135°	1
Cool	300°	150°	2
Warm	325°	165°	3
Moderate	350°	175°	4
Moderately hot	375°	190°	5
Fairly hot	400°	200°	6
Hot	425°	220°	7
Very hot	450°	230°	8
Very hot	475°	245°	9

COMMON INGREDIENTS AND THEIR APPROXIMATE EQUIVALENTS

1 cup uncooked white rice = 185 grams
1 cup all-purpose flour = 140 grams
1 stick butter (4 ounces • 1/2 cup • 8 tablespoons) = 110 grams
1 cup butter (8 ounces • 2 sticks • 16 tablespoons) = 220 grams
1 cup brown sugar, firmly packed = 225 grams
1 cup granulated sugar = 200 grams

Information compiled from a variety of sources, including *Recipes into Type* by Joan Whitman and Dolores Simon (Newton, MA: Biscuit Books, 2000); *The New Food Lover's Companion* by Sharon Tyler Herbst (Hauppauge, NY: Barron's, 1995); and *Rosemary Brown's Big Kitchen Instruction Book* (Kansas City, MO: Andrews McMeel, 1998).

INDEX